T0354372

Chelsea's
GLUTEN FREE COOKBOOK

Everyday recipes you love, Now Gluten Free

Chelsea R. Wink

iUniverse, Inc.
New York   Bloomington

Chelsea's Gluten Free Cookbook
Everyday recipes you love, Now Gluten Free

Copyright © 2010 Chelsea R. Wink

iUniverse books may be ordered through booksellers or by contacting:

iUniverse
1663 Liberty Drive
Bloomington, IN 47403
www.iuniverse.com
1-800-Authors (1-800-288-4677)

ISBN: 978-1-4502-3169-5 (pbk)
ISBN: 978-1-4502-3170-1 (ebk)

Printed in the United States of America

iUniverse rev. date: 6/3/2010

For Brian

Contents

Preface

When someone receives the diagnosis of Celiac Disease, life changes forever. Everything that person consumes must now be completely gluten free. That doesn't mean sometimes or when one feels like it; it means from now on. There are no cheat days and no exceptions. They now must create a new normal that involves never consuming foods containing gluten, in any form, again.

The simple task of stopping to pick-up a couple of burgers on the way home is no longer possible. Just running out to grab a bite is now a chore that includes great planning and a lot more time! Your meals out become a lesson in logistics and availability and then you must trust that there is no cross contamination with your gluten free choice as well. What a nightmare!

This is why I wrote "Chelsea's Gluten Free Cookbook". I am the wife of a Celiac and when my husband was first diagnosed, our life turned upside down. Now, after studying, researching, and testing lots of foods and recipes, we are surviving and happy in our new normal and I hope this cookbook helps you create your new normal too.

I met my husband, Brian, in 2003. We met through mutual friends, and hit it off right away. We dated for a year and everything was great, but I started to notice that as soon as we would eat, Brian would have to rush off to the restroom. His condition continued to worsen and it started affecting our everyday lives. Brian was starting to complain of severe stomach pains, and was not eating much. My mentality was to give him saltine crackers (big mistake), and sandwiches on wheat bread (even bigger mistake).

A couple of months before our wedding, Brian was losing weight at a rapid pace. After much complaining on my part, I convinced him to see a doctor. After seeing a gastroenterologist, a colonoscopy was scheduled. The results came back and they told us his problems were gone forever. However, Brian's symptoms were not gone and he continued to lose weight. Our wedding was quickly approaching and, no offense to my sweet husband, but he was starting to look really sick. His eyes were starting to get dark rings, his cheeks were sinking in and his skin tone looked different. So, again, I insisted he see another doctor. This doctor told us that Brian's problem was either IBS or cancer. Unfortunately, misdiagnosis for the celiac is a common occurrence. Obviously, we decided to get a third opinion. *This is probably starting to sound familiar isn't it?*

We finally found a doctor who was willing to really research Brian's problem. Tests were run, biopsies were performed, and the doctor actually interviewed Brian to better understand his problems. What a concept!

One week later, Brian was told he has Celiac Disease and would have to start living a completely Gluten Free diet. I had never even heard of gluten, and had no idea where it came from or what it did. I feared my sweet brand new husband Brian would never eat again!

Luckily that didn't happen! We studied the disease, its etiology and what we could do to eliminate the symptoms Brian was experiencing. We researched how to cook gluten free and how to start living a gluten free lifestyle. I then realized that I would have to learn how to cook!

I used to burn an entire loaf of bread trying to make one grilled cheese sandwich and gourmet cooking, in our house came from a microwave, probably like most young couples. But, I loved Brian and I was going to do everything in my power to make sure he would eat gluten free. I wanted him to be able to eat his favorite dishes, have deserts, and live a normal life. This is where we discovered our new normal!

I work constantly to stay up-to-date on research and aware of innovations in gluten free foods. I have also started, as I am sure you will too, educating friends and family about eating gluten free. I am by no means an expert; I am however, the wife of a celiac with lots of experience preparing gluten-free meals and I like them too.

Chelsea Wink

*All ingredients used in this book are Gluten Free. Please check all your labels and make sure your ingredients are Gluten Free. If you are not sure about any ingredients, it is better to stay away.

All gluten intolerant people are different; some ingredients may affect others differently.

What is gluten?

Gluten is defined as a cohesive, elastic protein that is left behind after starch is washed away from wheat flour dough. Gluten is made up of many different proteins. The main protein is gliadin. Upon digestion, the gluten proteins break down into peptides, or polypeptide chains, that are made up of strings of amino acids. The parent proteins have polypeptide chains that include hundreds of amino acids. There is one peptide in particular that has been shown to be harmful to those with celiac disease. This peptide includes 19 amino acids strung together in a specific sequence. Even though this peptide proves to be harmful, there are other peptides that may be harmful also.

It is certain that there are polypeptide chains in barley and rye. Oats have a similar, but not exact, polypeptide chain. Oats are currently controversial because there is scientific proof proving both sides.

What is celiac disease?

Celiac disease is a genetically linked lifelong digestive disorder that affects people of all ages. When those with celiac disease eat the protein gluten, an autoimmune response is set off to attack the villi, the tiny hair like lining in the small intestines. This prevents the small intestines from gaining any type of nutrients. If celiac disease is left untreated, damage to the small bowel can be chronic and life threatening. This will lead to several complications, including:

- Iron deficiency anemia
- Osteoporosis
- Vitamin deficiency
- Pancreatic insufficiency
- Type 1 diabetes
- Thyroid disease
- Dermatitis Herpetiformis (DH)

Celiac disease may appear at any age. It can be triggered from anything from a surgery or emotional stress to infection or pregnancy. Symptoms of celiac disease are extremely varied and do not always affect the digestive system. Some symptoms may include:

- Recurring bloating, gas, or abdominal pain
- Chronic diarrhea , constipation, or both
- Unexplained weight loss or gain
- Pale, foul smelling stool
- Unexplained anemia
- Bone or joint pain

- Depression
- Vitamin K deficiency
- Fatigue or lack of energy
- Delayed growth or onset of puberty
- Missed menstrual periods
- Infertility: male & female
- Miscarriages
- Canker sores
- Tooth discoloration

In infants, toddlers and young children some more subtle symptoms may be:

- Failure to thrive (infants)
- Growth failure
- Vomiting
- Bloating
- Behavioral changes

Approximately 1 out of 133 people have celiac disease but only 3% have been diagnosed.

In order to be properly diagnosed with celiac disease, the individual must be eating gluten. Certain blood tests will be drawn to determine if there is a presence of celiac disease. If the antibody shows up in the blood test, it is imperative to have a small bowel biopsy. This procedure, performed endoscopically, will confirm diagnosis of celiac disease.

Eating gluten free

Since celiac disease is a chronic autoimmune disorder, a gluten free diet is the only solution. When gluten is removed from the diet, the villi in the small intestines will start to heal as well as the overall health of the individual.

Adhering to a gluten free lifestyle can be difficult. The individual must learn how to read labels and learn how to spot potential harmful ingredients such as:

- Unidentified starches
- Binders
- Fillers
- Extenders
- Malt

Many labels, however, do not simply state "contains gluten" or "gluten free". The following list contains products containing gluten as well as products you would least expect to find gluten.

- Alcohol made from grains
- Barley
- Bran
- Canned meat- containing preservatives
- Canned vegetables- excluding those in water only
- Cereal
- Cheese spread
- Dips
- Gum
- Fruit drinks

- Instant hot drinks- coffee, tea, chocolate
- Ketchups
- Lunch meat
- Malt
- Monosodium Glutamate
- Mustards
- Oats
- Rye
- Salad dressings
- Sauces
- Sausages
- Seasoning mixes
- Soups
- Soy sauce
- Starch
- Wheat flour
- White pepper

The above list does have gluten free substitutes. Most products can be found gluten free; however, you may spend a little bit more time at the grocery store.

The following recipes are, obviously, gluten free. However, make sure to read packages and labels to assure the ingredients you buy are, in fact, gluten free. The recipes have been tested on a diagnosed celiac, but I cannot be responsible for cross contamination occurring in stores or homes.

APPETIZERS & BREADS

Almond Dip

Artichoke Dip

Asparagus Dip

Bread

Bruschetta

Cheese Ball

Chicken Salad Dip

Chunky Salsa

Cornbread Dressing

Corn Tortillas

Deviled Eggs

Fruit Dip

Guacamole

Lettuce Wraps

Pumpkin Muffins

Spinach & Artichoke Dip

Stuffed Mushrooms

Sun-Dried Tomato Dip

Almond Dip

⅓ C Almonds, sliced
2 pkg Cream cheese, whipped
1 TBS Milk
½ tsp Garlic powder
½ tsp Onion powder
¼ tsp Oregano
⅛ tsp Basil
¼ tsp Salt
¼ tsp Pepper

Set oven to 350°.

Spread the almonds onto a baking sheet. Cook for 5-10 minutes, until lightly roasted.

Beat all other ingredients together until evenly mixed.

Mix in the almonds just before serving.

Serve with crackers or vegetables.

Artichoke Dip

16 oz Mozzarella cheese, shredded
1 C Parmesan cheese
1 C Mayonnaise
1 Can Artichoke hearts, drained and chopped
1 Red pepper, finely chopped
4 Garlic cloves, minced

Set oven to 250°.

Mix all ingredients together in a large mixing bowl.

Transfer to an 8x8 baking dish then cook for 1 hour.

Serve with crackers, chips, or vegetables.

Asparagus Dip

1 Bunch Asparagus spears
3 TBS Olive oil
1½ C Mayonnaise
1½ C Parmesan cheese
2 Garlic cloves, minced

Set oven to 350°.

Sauté the asparagus with the olive oil until tender.

Place the asparagus in a large bowl and mash evenly.

Add the mayonnaise, Parmesan cheese, and garlic to the asparagus and mix well.

Transfer to an 8x8 baking dish and cook for 20-30 minutes.

Bread

½ C Arrowroot
½ C Tapioca starch
1 C Potato flour
1 C Corn starch
1 C Rice four
1 Pkt Yeast
¾ tsp Xanthan gum
1 TBS Baking powder
1 tsp Baking soda
2 tsp Sugar
½ tsp Salt
6 TBS Shortening
¾ C Milk

Set oven to 375°.

Grease a shallow glass loaf pan.

Mix all dry ingredients together. Add the shortening and mix for 2 minutes. Blend in the milk and stir for an additional 2 minutes, using the dough hook if possible.

Place the dough in the loaf pan, cover with a towel, and set in a warm place for 20 minutes to allow the bread to rise.

Cook the bread for 25-30 minutes.

Serve warm with a roasted garlic dipping sauce.

Bruschetta

7 Plum tomatoes, ripe
3 Garlic cloves, minced
1½ TBS Extra virgin olive oil
1 tsp Balsamic vinegar
8-10 Basil leaves, fresh and finely chopped
Salt to taste
Pepper to taste

In a large saucepan, boil 6-8 cups of water. Remove from heat and immediately submerge the tomatoes into the water. Let sit for 1-2 minutes. Drain.

Remove the skins of the tomatoes using a small paring knife. Cut each peeled tomato into quarters and remove the seeds and juices from the center.

Finely chop the tomatoes and place in a medium bowl. Add the garlic, extra virgin olive oil, balsamic vinegar, and basil leaves and mix. Add the salt and pepper to taste and mix well.

Serve with any gluten free crackers or bread.

Cheese Ball

2 pkg Cream cheese, softened
1 can Crushed pineapple, drained
¼ C Bell peppers, finely chopped
2 TBS Onions, minced
1 TBS Seasoned salt
2 C Pecans, finely chopped

Mix all ingredients together. Form into 2 balls, wrap in plastic wrap, and refrigerate for 2 hours before serving.

Serve with crackers or fruit.

Chicken Salad Dip

4 C Chicken, cooked and finely chopped
3 pkg Cream cheese, softened
½ C Coconut flakes, toasted
4 Celery stalks, finely chopped
6 Scallions, finely chopped
¼ C Almonds, finely chopped and toasted
1 TBS Curry powder
1 tsp Salt
½ tsp Pepper
1 TBS Ginger root, freshly grated

In a large bowl, combine the all ingredients. Stir until well mixed.

Shape into a ball or shape and place on a plate. Refrigerate at least 1 hour before serving.

Chunky Salsa

6 Anaheim peppers, seeds removed and finely chopped
1 Pasilla chili, seeds removed and finely chopped
1 Jalapeno, seeds removed and finely chopped
1 Onion, finely chopped
Juice of 1 lime
2 Cans Diced tomatoes, drained
1 tsp Garlic salt

Finely chop the anaheim peppers, the pasilla chili, and the jalapeno. Place in a medium bowl and stir together. Chop and add the onion to the salsa. Stir in the lime juice, garlic salt, and tomatoes.

Serve immediately. The salsa may be refrigerated for up to a week.

Cornbread Dressing

8 pkg Gluten free cornbread
2 C Chicken broth
4 Onions, diced
2 C Celery, chopped
1 Stick of butter
6 Eggs, beaten

Cook the cornbread according to the packages directions.

Sauté the onions and celery with butter in a large pan. Set oven to 350°.

Place 4 pans of cooled cornbread into a large bowl. Add 1 C of chicken broth. (More or less may be used to achieve the desired consistency) Add 3 of the beaten eggs and stir until the dressing is saturated. Add half of the caramelized onions and celery to the dressing and mix well. Repeat this step with the remaining ingredients.

Place each bowl of dressing into their own 9x13 baking dish. Spread the dressing evenly throughout the dish. Place 6-8 pats of butter randomly throughout the dressing.

Bake at 350° for 30 minutes. Serve immediately or refrigerate for next day servings.

*To make less dressing, only use half of the ingredients

Corn Tortillas

2 C Minsa® corn masa flour
1¼ C Boiling water
1¼ tsp Kosher salt
1 tsp Shortening

In a small saucepan, bring the water to a boil. Add the shortening.

In a large bowl, mix the corn masa and salt together.

Pour the boiling water into the corn masa mix. Let cool.

Once cooled, knead the dough together. More water or corn masa may be used to reach doughy consistency.

Separate the dough into golf ball size balls. Place each ball, separately, onto a tortilla press and flatten. If you don't have a tortilla press, use a rolling pin to roll the dough out.

Heat a cast iron skillet over medium heat. Place one tortilla in the skillet and cook for 45 seconds. Flip the tortilla and cook for an additional 45 seconds. Repeat this step until all of the dough is gone.

Store the tortillas in a tortilla warmer or in foil.

Deviled Eggs

6 Hard boiled eggs, peeled and cut lengthwise
¼ C Mayonnaise
1 tsp Mustard, spicy
½ tsp Vinegar
½ tsp Kosher salt
¼ tsp Pepper
Paprika for garnish
1 tsp Chives for garnish

Prepare the eggs.

Remove the yolks and place in a small bowl. Add mayonnaise, mustard, vinegar, salt, and pepper to the yolks and mash. Mix thoroughly.

Fill the eggs with the mixture. Garnish with paprika and chives.

Cover with plastic wrap at least 4 hours before serving.

Fruit Dip

1 pkg Cream cheese, softened
2 TBS Heavy cream
2 TBS Brown sugar
1 tsp Cinnamon
1 tsp Vanilla
¼ tsp Nutmeg

Mix all ingredients together. Refrigerate for an hour before serving.

Serve with fruit.

Guacamole

2 Avocados, peeled & pitted
1 tsp Garlic Salt
1 tsp Onion Powder
1 Can Diced tomatoes with green chilies, drained
½ Lime wedge

Place the avocados in a large bowl. Add the garlic salt, onion powder, tomatoes, and the juice from the lime wedge. Mash all ingredients until well mixed. Serve immediately.

Lettuce Wraps

2 Chicken breasts
2 TBS Olive oil
1 C Water chestnuts
1 C Mushrooms
4 TBS Onion, minced
1 C Bean sprouts
1 Garlic clove, minced
2 TBS Soy sauce
2 TBS Brown sugar
1 tsp Rice vinegar
1 TBS Olive oil
5-7 Iceberg lettuce leaves
Hoisin sauce, optional

Sauté the chicken breasts and olive oil, in a large skillet, over medium heat. Cook until the center of the chicken reaches 165°.

Remove the chicken from the pan but keep the oil hot.

Mince the chicken, water chestnuts, mushrooms, onion, bean sprouts, and garlic.

In a small bowl, mix together the soy sauce, brown sugar, and rice vinegar.

Add the other tablespoon of olive oil to the pan, along with the chicken, water chestnuts, mushrooms, onion, bean sprouts, and garlic. Stir in the sauce mixture.

Sauté for 10-15 minutes.

Place about 1/3 cup of the chicken mixture into each lettuce leaves. Hoisin sauce may be served with each lettuce wrap.

Pumpkin Muffins

1 C Gluten free all purpose flour
½ C Arrowroot
½ C Sugar
2 tsp Baking powder
1 tsp Cinnamon
½ tsp Ginger
¼ tsp Ground cloves
1 Egg, beaten
½ C Milk
½ C Canned pumpkin
4 TBS Butter, melted
2½ tsp Sugar
½ tsp Cinnamon

Set oven to 400°.

Sift the gluten free flour, arrowroot, ½ cup sugar, baking powder, cinnamon, ginger, and cloves in a large bowl.

In a separate bowl, mix the egg, milk, pumpkin, and melted butter. Gradually stir into the flour mixture.

Lightly grease the muffin pans and fill each ⅔ full of batter.

Mix 2½ tsp sugar and ½ tsp cinnamon together in a small bowl. Sprinkle on top of the unbaked muffins.

Cook for 20-25 minutes.

Spinach & Artichoke Dip

2 pkg Spinach, frozen chopped
½ C Onion, finely chopped
1 Can Artichoke hearts, drained and chopped
1 pkg Cream cheese, softened
16 oz Monterey Jack cheese, shredded
⅓ C Half & half

Set oven to 350°.

Defrost the spinach, pressing the excess moisture out.

Mix all ingredients together in a large mixing bowl. Pour into an 8x8 baking dish and cook for 25-30 minutes.

Serve immediately with crackers or gluten free bread.

Stuffed Mushrooms

20-25 Large mushrooms
4 TBS Butter
1 Onion, finely chopped
8 oz Mozzarella cheese, shredded
1 jar Bacon bits
¾ C Gluten free breadcrumbs

Set oven to 350°.

Remove the stems from the mushrooms and place in a large pan. Sauté the stems in the butter with the onion. Sauté until the onions turn a golden brown.

Remove from heat then add the mozzarella cheese, bacon bits, and gluten free breadcrumbs. Stir until evenly mixed.

Stuff the mixture into the tops of the mushrooms and place on a baking sheet. Cook for 30-35 minutes.

Serve immediately.

Sun-Dried Tomato Dip

1 pkg Cream cheese, softened
1 C Sharp cheddar cheese, shredded
¼ C Sun-dried tomatoes, chopped
½ tsp Garlic salt
¼ tsp Paprika
¼ tsp Salt

In a mixing bowl, beat the cream cheese, cheddar cheese, sun-dried tomatoes, garlic salt, paprika, and salt until well mixed.

Transfer to a serving bowl, cover, and chill at least 1 hour before serving.

Serve with gluten free crackers or bread.

BREAKFAST

Apple Cinnamon Quinoa

Banana Fritters

Breakfast Burritos

Breakfast Casserole

Breakfast Smoothie

Crustless Quiche

Egg and Cheese Casserole

Fruit and Yogurt Parfait

Granola

Hobo Breakfast

Potato Pancakes

Sausage & Potato Casserole

Apple Cinnamon Quinoa

1 C Quinoa, rinsed
2 C Apple juice
1 tsp Cinnamon
¼ tsp Nutmeg
2 Granny Smith apples, diced
1 C Dried cranberries
¼ C Pecans
1¼ C Yogurt

Cook the quinoa according to the packages directions.

When the quinoa is finished, remove from heat. Stir in the remaining ingredients.

This may be served hot or cold. Store in the refrigerator for up to 3 days.

Banana Fritters

1 pkg Gluten free pancake mix
2-3 Bananas, sliced
Powdered sugar for garnish

Prepare the pancake batter according to the packages directions.

Add all of the sliced bananas to the batter and fold into the mixture, making sure to evenly coat the bananas.

Place 8-12 bananas in a large skillet over medium heat for 4-6 minutes. Flip the fritters once and let cook for an additional 4-5 minutes.

Garnish with powdered sugar and serve immediately.

Breakfast Burritos

Corn tortillas
2 TBS Butter
1 Onion, chopped
1 Bell pepper, chopped
1 can Diced tomatoes, drained
4 Eggs
4 Egg whites
Salsa
¾ C Cheddar cheese, shredded

In a large skillet, add the butter and sauté, over medium heat, the onion and the bell pepper. Add the diced tomatoes, heat, and then set aside.

In a separate skillet, scramble the eggs and the egg whites.

Place the eggs and vegetables on a corn tortilla and top with salsa and/or cheese. Serve immediately.

Breakfast Casserole

2 C Gluten free breadcrumbs
4 TBS Butter, softened
1 lb Sausage, cooked and drained
8 oz Sharp cheddar cheese, shredded
5 Eggs, beaten
2 C Half & half
2 tsp Salt
1 tsp Basil
½ tsp Pepper

Place the breadcrumbs on the bottom of a 9x13 casserole dish. Sprinkle the sausage and cheddar cheese on top of the breadcrumbs.

Mix the eggs, half & half, salt, pepper, and basil together and beat well.

Pour evenly over the casserole.

Chill in the refrigerator overnight.

Bake at 350° for 40-50 minutes.

Breakfast Smoothie

1 Banana, frozen and sliced
2 TBS Yogurt
Juice of 1 orange
¼ C Pineapple
¼ C Blueberries
¼ C Raspberries
¼ C Strawberries
⅓ C Chopped nuts

In a blender, mix together the banana, the orange juice, and the yogurt.

Gradually add the rest of the ingredients, except the chopped nuts. Mix on high until there are no more lumps.

Transfer to the desired glass and top with the chopped nuts.

Crustless Quiche

5 Eggs
¼ C Arrowroot
½ tsp Baking powder
1 C Cottage cheese, small curd
2 C Monterey Jack cheese, shredded
4 TBS Butter
1 Onion, chopped
1 can Green chilies, chopped
½ lb Bacon, cooked and chopped
Salt and Pepper to taste

Set oven to 350°.

Grease a 9x13 casserole dish.

In a large bowl, beat the eggs, arrowroot, and baking powder. Gradually stir in the cottage cheese, Monterey Jack cheese, butter, onions, chilies, and bacon. Mix well, then add salt and pepper to taste.

Pour mixture into the casserole dish then bake for 35-40 minutes, or until set.

Serve immediately.

Egg and Cheese Casserole

3 C Gluten free breadcrumbs
12 Eggs
2 C Milk
2 tsp Salt
1 tsp Pepper
¾ tsp Onion powder
2 TBS Chives, chopped
2 C Cheddar cheese, shredded

Set the oven to 350°.

Place the gluten free breadcrumbs on the bottom of a greased 9x13 baking dish.

In a large bowl, whisk together the eggs, milk, salt, pepper, onion powder, and chives. Gradually stir in the cheese.

Pour the egg mixture over the breadcrumbs. Cover and refrigerate the casserole for at least 7 hours.

Uncover and stir, then cook for 30 minutes, or until set.

Serve immediately.

Fruit and Yogurt Parfait

¼ C Strawberries, sliced
¼ C Pineapple chunks
¼ C Raspberries
¼ C Kiwi, sliced
¼ C Grapes
1 C Yogurt
¼ C Granola

In a small bowl, combine all fruit.

Stir in the yogurt and mix well.

Sprinkle the granola on top of the fruit parfait and serve immediately.

Granola

4 C Gluten free oats
1 C Almonds, sliced
½ C Coconut
¼ Sunflower seeds, shelled
½ C Pure maple syrup
2 TBS Canola oil
½ tsp Salt
1 C Dried cherries

Set oven to 350°.

In a large bowl, combine the oats, almonds, coconut, and sunflower seeds. Stir in the maple syrup, canola oil, and salt.

Transfer to a baking dish and cook for 25 minutes, tossing once.

Remove the granola from the oven and stir in the dried cherries. Let cool.

Store granola in an airtight container.

Hobo Breakfast

6 Eggs
4 Potatoes, peeled and shredded
1 lb Cooked ham, chopped
1 Onion, chopped
2 C Sharp cheddar cheese, shredded
Butter
Salt to taste
Pepper to taste

Coat the inside of a large cooking foil bag with nonstick cooking spray. Sprinkle the salt and pepper on the foil and place small pats of butter on the bottom.

Beat the eggs in a bowl then transfer to a large zip lock bag. Place the shredded potatoes into the bag. Add the ham, onion, and cheese. Mix by squeezing the bag.

Pour the mixture into the foil cooking bag and spread evenly. Add more salt, pepper, and pats of butter to the mixture.

Double fold the bag to seal. Cook on a grill over medium heat, turning every 5 minutes. Check frequently to determine when the breakfast is done.

Potato Pancakes

4 Potatoes, peeled
4 Eggs, beaten
1 Onion, finely chopped
¼ C All purpose gluten free flour
1 tsp Salt
¼ C Vegetable oil

Shred the potatoes, rinse, drain, and pat dry.

Mix potatoes, eggs, onion, gluten free flour, and salt in a large bowl.

Heat 2 tablespoons of oil in a large skillet over medium heat. For each pancake, pour ¼ C potato batter into the skillet. Using a large spatula, flatten into the shape of a pancake.

Cook pancakes for 3 minutes on each side or until golden brown. Cover to keep warm while the remaining pancakes are being cooked. Repeat until there is no more batter. Add oil as needed to prevent sticking.

Serve immediately with maple syrup.

Sausage & Potato Casserole

1 lb Sausage, cooked and drained
3½ C Potatoes, shredded
1½ C Sharp cheddar cheese, shredded
1¼ C Milk
7 Eggs, beaten
1 can Green chilies
2 tsp Salt
½ tsp Pepper

Set oven to 350°.

In a large mixing bowl, add the sausage, potatoes, cheese, milk, eggs, and green chilies. Mix well. Add the salt and pepper.

Transfer to a 9x13 baking dish and cook for 1 hour.

Serve immediately.

Desserts

Apple Crisp

Butter Cream Icing

Carrot Cake

Chex® Mix

Chocolate Chess Pie

Coconut Bars

Cool Cookies

Cream Cheese Icing

Double Chocolate

Peanut Butter Brownies

Fruit Parfait

Mint Chocolate Chip Cookies

Pecan Pie

Pineapple Upside Down Cake

Peanut Butter Cookies

Pie Crust

Roasted Pear

Apple Crisp

4 C Granny Smith apples, peeled and thinly sliced
½ C Brown sugar
1 TBS Cinnamon
2 TBS and ½ C All Purpose Gluten Free flour
2 C Gluten Free oatmeal
¼ C Sugar
½ C Butter, melted

Set oven to 350°.

In a large bowl, place the apples, brown sugar, cinnamon, and 2 TBS of gluten free flour. Stir until all apples are evenly coated. Place apples into a greased 8x8 dish.

In a separate bowl, mix together the oatmeal, ½ cup gluten free flour, sugar, and melted butter. Mixture will be crumbly.

Place the oatmeal topping on top of the apples. Spread evenly.

Bake for 45 minutes. Serve immediately.

Butter Cream Icing

3 C Powdered sugar
⅓ C Butter, softened
3 TBS Milk
2 tsp Vanilla

Mix together the powdered sugar and butter. Add the milk and vanilla. Beat until the icing reaches the desired consistency. More or less milk may be added to change the consistency.

Spread on any desired gluten free cake.

Carrot Cake

1 box Gluten Free yellow cake mix
4 Eggs
1¼ C Vegetable oil
¼ C Water
3 tsp Cinnamon
2 C Carrots, grated

Set oven to 350°.

Put the cake mix in a large mixing bowl. Beat in the eggs, then vegetable oil, then the water, cinnamon, and carrots. Beat until evenly mixed.

Transfer to a 9x9 baking dish.

Cook for 30-35 minutes.

Serve with cream cheese icing.

Chex® Mix

4½ C Corn Chex®
4½ C Rice Chex®
2 C Gluten free pretzels
1 C Mixed nuts
4 TBS Butter, melted
3 TBS Worcestershire sauce
½ tsp Garlic salt
½ tsp Onion powder

In a large bowl, mix together the corn Chex®, rice Chex®, pretzels, and mixed nuts.

Melt the butter in a small bowl and then add the Worcestershire sauce, garlic salt, and onion powder.

Drizzle the sauce over the Chex® mix and stir until evenly coated.

Microwave, uncovered, for 4 minutes, stirring every minute.

Place the mix on wax paper to cool. Store in an airtight container.

Chocolate Chess Pie

1 bag Chocolate chips
1 stick Butter, softened
1 C Sugar
2 Eggs
½ C All purpose gluten free flour
1 Gluten free pie crust

Set oven to 350°.

Place the chocolate chips on the bottom of the pie crust.

In a large bowl, mix together the butter, sugar, eggs, and gluten free flour. Pour the mixture into the pie crust.

Cook for 40-50 minutes.

Coconut Bars

1 box Gluten free white cake mix
1 stick Butter
¼ C Milk
1 bag Coconut
1 jar Caramel topping
¼ C All purpose gluten free flour

Set oven to 350°.

In a large mixing bowl, mix the cake mix, butter, and milk until crumbly. Set aside ¾ C of the mixture. Pack the rest of the mix into a greased 9x13 baking dish.

Cook for 15 minutes.

Remove the dish from the oven, and then sprinkle the coconut over the crust.

In a small sauce pan, heat the caramel and gluten free flour to boiling. Drizzle evenly over the coconut then sprinkle the ¾ C of mixture on top of the bars.

Bake for 20-25 minutes.

Cut into desired squares or bars and serve.

Cool Cookies

2 C Sugar
¼ C Cocoa
½ C Milk
¼ C Butter
1 Tsp vanilla
1 Pinch salt
¾ C Peanut butter
3 C Gluten Free oats

In a large saucepan, stir in sugar, cocoa, milk, butter, vanilla, and salt. Stir constantly over medium/low heat. When boiling, stir in peanut butter and oats. Stir thoroughly.

Place 1 spoonful of cookie mix onto wax paper. Repeat this until mixture is gone. Let set until hard.

Cream Cheese Icing

1 stick Butter, softened
1 C Powdered sugar
2 tsp Vanilla
1 pkg Cream cheese, softened
¼ tsp Salt
1 C Pecans, chopped

Mix all ingredients together in a large mixing bowl.

Frost your choice of cake.

Double Chocolate Peanut Butter Brownies

1 Box Gluten Free brownie mix- butter and eggs as called for on the box
20 Reese's miniatures

Set oven to 325°.

Make the brownie mix according to the boxes directions. Add 10 Reese's miniatures (whole) to the batter. Mix well; batter will be chunky.

Place brownies in a greased 8x8 pan. Place the remaining Reese's miniatures in the brownie batter.

Cook according to the packages directions.

Let brownies cool before serving.

Fruit Parfait

3 C sliced strawberries
1 pkg blueberries
1 pkg blackberries
2 C seedless grapes
2 C watermelon, balled
2 C cantaloupe, balled
1 C chocolate chips
whip cream

Wash all fruit.

Prepare all fruit, as mentioned above, and mix together in a large bowl.

In a sundae glass, martini glass, or something similar, place a small handful (about 6-10 pieces) of chocolate chips, then add a spoonful of the mixed fruit to the glass. Repeat this process until the glass is full. Top with whip cream and chocolate chips.

Serve immediately or place in refrigerator until ready to eat.

Mint Chocolate Chip Cookies

3 Egg whites
¼ tsp Cream of tartar
¼ tsp Salt
1 C Sugar
1½ tsp Vanilla
1 bag Mint chocolate chips

Set oven to 350°.

Beat the egg whites, cream of tartar, and salt until firm. Slowly beat in the sugar until the mix is shiny. Add the vanilla and the mint chocolate chips.

On an ungreased cookie sheet, drop the dough by tablespoons.

Cook for 20 minutes.

Pecan Pie

4 TBS Butter, softened
1 C Sugar
4 Eggs
¾ C Light corn syrup
1½ C Pecan halves
1 Gluten free pie crust

Set oven to 350°.

In a large bowl mix together the butter, sugar, eggs, and corn syrup. Gradually stir in the pecan halves.

Transfer the pie filling to the pie crust.

Cook for 45-55 minutes.

Pineapple Upside Down Cake

1 can Pineapple chunks, drained
1 can Cherries, pitted, drained
1 C Brown sugar
½ tsp Cinnamon
1 pkg Gluten free cake mix

Set oven to 350°.

In a large bowl, mix together the pineapples, cherries, and brown sugar. Set aside.

Prepare cake mix according to the packages directions and add the cinnamon.

Grease an 8x8 cake pan. Pour the fruit into the pan. Next, pour the cake batter over the fruit.

Cook for 40 minutes.

Let the cake cool before you serve.

Peanut Butter Cookies

2 Sticks Butter, softened
2 C Peanut Butter
1½ C Brown sugar, packed
1 Egg
½ C Arrowroot

Set oven to 325°.

Mix the butter, peanut butter, brown sugar, and egg on low for 1 minute. Gradually beat in the arrowroot until well mixed.

Roll the dough into walnut sized balls and place on greased cookie sheet.

Bake for 13-15 minutes. Do not overcook! Let cookies cool completely before removing from the cookie sheet.

Pie Crust

---

1 Pkg Gluten Free graham crackers, finely crushed
6 TBS Butter, melted ·
1 tsp Vanilla
¼ C Brown sugar

Set oven to 350°.

Mix all ingredients together in a large bowl or mixer.

In a pie pan, evenly spread the crust in the pan, making sure it isn't too thin. Smooth out the crust and cook for 30 minutes.

Fill with your desired choice of pie filling.

Roasted Pear

1 Pear
¼ C Water
½ tsp Cinnamon
⅔ C Fresh raspberries
1 Mint leaf
¼ C Pistachios, chopped
¼ C Chocolate chips

Set oven to 300°.

Cut the pear in half. Using a melon baller, remove the center of each half.

In a shallow casserole dish, stir together the water and cinnamon. Place the pears; face down, in the dish. Bake for 30 minutes, or until the pear is tender.

Meanwhile, puree the raspberries and the mint leaf. Strain the sauce to remove the raspberry seeds.

Once tender, remove the pears from the oven. Place the pears in a small dessert dish or martini glass. Fill each shallow center with chocolate chips and pistachios. Drizzle the raspberry sauce over the pears and top with the remaining chocolate chips and pistachios.

Serve immediately.

Fish & Shellfish

Ahi Tuna Rolls

Chili Lime Tilapia

Coconut Shrimp

Coconutty Mahi-Mahi

Crispy Shrimp

Fish Tacos

Ginger Salmon

Margarita Shrimp

Pecan Crusted Tilapia

Salmon Rub

Seafood Alfredo

Seafood Enchiladas

Shrimp Scampi

Tilapia in a Bag

Tuna Casserole

Ahi Tuna Rolls

5-6 Nori sheets
8 oz Sashimi grade ahi tuna
2 C Sushi rice, uncooked
4 TBS Rice vinegar
2 tsp Sugar
2 tsp Kosher salt
1 Avocado, cut into strips
1 Cucumber, cut into strips
½ pkg Cream cheese, sliced
Sesame seeds
Wasabi
Ginger, pickled and sliced
Bamboo sushi roller

Rinse the rice in cold water until the water runs clear.

Steam the rice in 2 cups of water in either a rice cooker or a sauce pan on the stove.

Meanwhile, heat the vinegar, sugar, and salt in a small saucepan over low heat. Do not boil. Cook until the sugar and salt is dissolved then remove from heat.

When the rice has finished cooking, add the vinegar mixture. Transfer the rice to a wooden bowl to let cool.

Slice the ahi tuna into thin strips.

Ahi Tuna Rolls
Continued

Place a sheet of nori on the bamboo sushi roller, shiny side down. Spread a thin layer of sushi rice on the nori. Place 2-3 strips of avocado, 2-4 strips of cucumber, 2-3 slices of cream cheese, and 2-3 slices of tuna onto one end of the nori.

Place your thumbs on the back of the mat and begin rolling away from you. Support the rest of the sushi filling with your hands. Using your hands, shape the roll.

Remove the bamboo sushi mat and slice the sushi roll into 6-8 pieces.

Serve with soy sauce, wasabi, and/or ginger.

Chili Lime Tilapia

2 Tilapia filets
2 Limes; juice
2 TBS olive oil
1 Tsp chili powder

Set oven to 350°

Mix the lime juice, olive oil, and chili powder in a large zip lock bag. Mix well. Place tilapia filets in bag and let marinade for 10 minutes.

Place filets in baking filet and cook for 25 minutes.

Serve immediately.

*Any type of fish may be used

Coconut Shrimp with Pina Colada Dipping Sauce

1 lb Shrimp, cooked and deveined
½ C Arrowroot
⅓ C Coconut rum
1 tsp Kosher salt
½ tsp Pepper
1½ C Coconut, shredded
1-2 C Organic vegetable shortening
1 C Pina colada mix
1 TBS Crushed pineapple, drained
2 tsp Coconut, shredded
1 TBS Corn starch

In a medium bowl, combine the arrowroot, coconut rum, kosher salt, and pepper. Stir well.

Add the shrimp to the batter and stir until all shrimp are evenly coated. Let sit for 10-15 minutes.

Place the coconut in a large bowl. Transfer the shrimp to the coconut and make sure the shrimp is evenly covered with coconut.

Coconut Shrimp
Continued

In a large skillet, over medium heat, melt the organic vegetable shortening.

Add the shrimp and cook until the shrimp is lightly browned.

Serve immediately with pina colada dipping sauce.

Mix the pina colada mix, crushed pineapple, coconut, and corn starch in a small bowl until well blended. Transfer to a serving bowl and serve immediately.

Coconutty Mahi-Mahi

2 TBS Kikkoman Soy Sauce
½ C Unsweetened coconut milk
4 C Water
3 Lemongrass stalks, crushed
5 Bay leaves
2 TBS Ginger, peeled and minced
¼ tsp Cayenne pepper
10 Shiitake mushrooms, stems removed
1 TBS Thai red curry paste
Lettuce leaves, for the bamboo steamer
4 Mahi-Mahi filets
Salt and pepper to taste

Pour soy sauce, coconut milk, and water into a large pot (same diameter as the bamboo steamer) and bring to a boil. Reduce heat to simmer then add the lemongrass, bay leaves, ginger, cayenne pepper, mushrooms, and curry paste. Simmer for 15 minutes.

Arrange the lettuce in the bamboo steamer to prevent the fish from touching the bamboo. Season the filets with salt and pepper then place into the bamboo steamer. Place the steamer on top of the pot and steam over medium/low heat for 30-40 minutes.

Remove the steamer from the pot. Using tongs, remove the bay leaves and lemongrass. Place the filets on the desired plates. Divide the mushrooms and sauce evenly over the filets and serve immediately with onion rice.

*Any type of fish may be used

Crispy Shrimp

¼ C Sorghum
¼ C Cornmeal
¼ tsp Paprika
¼ tsp Cayenne pepper
¼ tsp Basil
½ tsp Salt
Pepper to taste
¾ lb Cooked shrimp, detailed and deveined
2 Eggs

In a small bowl, whisk together the sorghum, cornmeal, paprika, cayenne pepper, basil, salt, and pepper.

In a separate small bowl, beat together the 2 eggs.

Dip the shrimp in the eggs then into the flour mixture, making sure the shrimp is evenly coated.

In a skillet, cook the shrimp in ½ inch of olive oil. Cook for 2-3 minutes, or until shrimp turns a golden brown.

Serve immediately with tartar sauce.

Fish Tacos

1 lb Mahi Mahi, cut into fillets
¼ C Extra virgin olive oil
Juice of 2 limes
1 TBS Lime zest
¼ C Cilantro, chopped
1 TBS Cayenne pepper
Toppings:
White cabbage, shredded
Salsa
Sour cream
Cilantro, chopped
Red onion, sliced
Corn tortillas

Preheat grill to medium heat.

Place the fillets in a shallow baking dish. Whisk together the olive oil, lime juice, lime zest, cilantro, and cayenne pepper. Pour the sauce over the fish, making sure to evenly coat the fish. Let marinate for 30 minutes.

Place the fish on the grill, flesh side down, and cook for 4-5 minutes. Turn once and cook for 1 minute. Remove from grill and let cool. Check by flaking the fish with a fork.

Divide the fish amongst the corn tortillas and top each taco with your choice of toppings.

Ginger Salmon

4 Salmon fillets
2 TBS Gingerroot, thinly sliced
2 TBS Scallions, chopped
1 TBS Soy sauce
Olive oil

Set oven to 350°.

Arrange the salmon in a 9x13 casserole dish. Sprinkle the gingerroot and scallions on top of the salmon. Splash the soy sauce over the fillets.

Cook for 15 minutes, or until the fish flakes easily.

Serve with cucumber pineapple salsa or kiwi salsa.

Margarita Shrimp

1½ lbs Large uncooked shrimp, peeled and deveined
⅓ C Lime juice
¼ C Tequila
¼ C Water
¼ Onion, diced
2 TBS Olive oil
Salt to taste
2 Limes, sliced
Skewers

Place the shrimp in a small marinating container.

In a separate bowl, mix the lime juice, tequila, water, onion, and olive oil. Pour the marinade over the shrimp, making sure to coat shrimp evenly, and set aside for 10 minutes.

Place the marinated shrimp onto the skewers, making enough for the amount of servings you need.

Place the remaining marinade into a small saucepan and bring to a boil then simmer for 5 minutes. Keep over low heat to keep the marinade warm.

Heat the grill to medium low. Place the shrimp skewers on for 3-4 minutes for each side, careful to not overcook.

Remove from grill. Serve over rice, drizzle the marinade over the shrimp and rice, and garnish with lime.

Pecan Crusted Tilapia

4 Tilapia fillets
1 C Pecans, finely chopped
¼ C Gluten free bread crumbs
2 tsp Lemon zest
Juice of 1 lemon
1 Egg
1 TBS Milk
1 tsp Salt
¼ tsp Pepper
2 TBS Olive oil

In a medium bowl, mix the pecans, gluten free bread crumbs, and lemon zest. In a separate bowl, whisk together the lemon juice, egg, and milk.

Sprinkle all of the fillets with the salt and pepper. Dip each fillet into the egg mixture, making sure to evenly coat the fish. Then dip the fillet into the pecan mixture, making sure each fillet is entirely covered with the pecan mixture.

Heat a large skillet over medium heat and add the olive oil, then add the fish. Reduce heat to medium low. Cook 10 minutes, turning once carefully. Fish will flake easily with a fork when done.

Serve immediately.

Salmon Rub

1 tsp White wine vinegar
1 tsp Garlic salt
1 tsp Italian seasoning
½ tsp Oregano
¼ tsp Celery salt

Set oven to 325°.

Mix all dry ingredients together in a small bowl. Add the vinegar and stir well.

Using your hands, rub the seasoning evenly on to the salmon.

Place in a shallow baking dish and cook for 30 minutes. Serve immediately.

*Any type of fish may be used

Seafood Alfredo

1 pkg Gluten Free linguine
2 TBS Butter
½ lb Medium cooked shrimp, detailed
½ lb Small bay scallops
½ tsp Minced garlic
1 can Quartered artichoke hearts, drained
1½ C Fresh whole Portobello mushrooms
1 jar Classico Mushroom Alfredo Sauce
Parmesan Cheese to garnish
Parsley to garnish

Cook the linguine according to the packages directions.

Meanwhile, sauté the shrimp, scallops, and garlic in the butter for 10 minutes.

In a separate bowl, stir the artichokes and mushrooms together.

Add the artichokes and mushrooms and the Alfredo sauce to the seafood mix and sauté for an additional 10 minutes.

Drain pasta and return to pot. Pour the creamy seafood into the pasta and stir until evenly coated.

Serve immediately and garnish with Parmesan cheese and parsley.

Seafood Enchiladas

6-8 Corn tortillas
½ lb Crab meat, fresh
¼ lb Shrimp, cooked, detailed, deveined, and chopped
1 Onion, chopped
3 TBS Butter
1 C Mozzarella cheese, shredded
1 C Half and half
¾ C Sour cream
¼ C Butter, melted
1 Garlic clove, minced
2 tsp Parsley
Salt and pepper to taste

Set oven to 350°.

In a large skillet, sauté the onion with 3 tablespoons of butter until caramelized.

Remove from heat and stir in the crab meat and shrimp. Stir in ½ cup of mozzarella cheese.

Place a heaping spoonful of mixture into each tortilla. Roll the tortilla and place in a 9x13 casserole dish. Repeat steps until all mixture is gone.

In a medium saucepan heat the half and half, sour cream, butter, garlic, and parsley. Stir until the mixture is well blended.

Pour the sauce over the enchiladas. Sprinkle the remaining ½ cup of mozzarella cheese over the enchiladas.

Cook for 30-35 minutes. Serve immediately.

Shrimp Scampi

½ C Butter
¼ lb. Cooked shrimp, detailed & deveined
1 Garlic clove, minced
1 tsp Parsley
½ tsp Pepper
½ tsp Onion powder

In a large skillet, sauté the butter and the garlic with the parsley, pepper, and onion powder. Add the shrimp and sauté for 8 minutes. Remove from heat and serve immediately.

Use the remaining butter for dipping sauce.

Tilapia in a Bag

4 TBS Extra virgin olive oil
1 C Coconut milk
4 Tilapia fillets
1 TBS Fresh ginger, peeled and grated
1 TBS Lemon zest
Juice of 1 lemon
½ bag Frozen snow peas
4 Yukon gold potatoes, cubed
1 tsp Salt
Parchment paper

Set oven to 350°.

In a large resealable bag, mix the olive oil, coconut milk, ginger, lemon zest, and lemon juice. Add the tilapia filets. Shake well, assuring all filets are evenly coated. Set aside.

Tear off the parchment paper every 1½ ft. Remove the tilapia from the bag and place 1 tilapia per parchment paper.

Divide the snow peas 4 ways and place them on top of the tilapia. Place 1 cubed potato, per pouch, on the tilapia.

Fold the parchment paper so that nothing can escape the pouch.

Transfer pouches to a baking sheet and cook for 10-15 minutes or until the fish flakes easily and the potatoes are tender.

Serve immediately.

Tuna Casserole

1 C Lays potato chips, crushed
1¼ C Uncooked gluten free pasta shells
3 TBS Butter
2 TBS Arrowroot
1 tsp Salt
2 C Milk
1 C Sharp cheddar cheese, shredded
2 C Fresh broccoli or 1 C Frozen broccoli
2 cans Tuna drained

Set oven to 325°.

Cook and drain pasta according to the packages directions.

While pasta is cooking, melt the butter in a medium saucepan over low heat. Stir in arrowroot and salt. Cook over medium heat until smooth, and then remove from heat. Gradually stir in the milk, then heat to boiling. Stir in cheese and remove from heat.

In an ungreased casserole dish, mix the pasta, broccoli, tuna, and sauce together. Cover and cook for 30 minutes or until bubbly.

Sprinkle the crushed chips on top of the casserole and cook for an additional 5 minutes, uncovered.

Serve immediately.

MEATS: BEEF & PORK

Beef & Broccoli Stir Fry

Beef Stroganoff

Beef Tamales

Beef Tenderloin with Horseradish Sauce

Chicken Fried Steak

Hobo Dinner

Lemon Rosemary Pork Tenderloin

Pineapple Ginger Ribs

Pineapple Glazed Ham

Pot Roast

Pulled Pork

Roasted Pork Tenderloin

Shepherd's Pie

Slow Cooked Pork Ribs

Southwest Pork Chops with Corn Salsa

Taco Meat

Taco Wrap

Beef & Broccoli Stir Fry

1 lb Beef stew meat
½ Medium onion
1 Can sliced mushrooms
1 Bag frozen broccoli stir fry mix
¼ C Worcestershire sauce
1 tsp Garlic salt
½ C Water
2 C Cooked rice
Pepper to taste

In a large wok or skillet, add the Worcestershire sauce and the beef. Cook over medium heat, stirring occasionally, for 15 minutes.

Next add the onion, mushrooms, broccoli stir fry mix, garlic salt, pepper, and water into the wok or skillet. Stir until everything is evenly mixed.

Simmer over medium/low heat for 15 minutes.

Serve immediately over rice.

Beef Stroganoff

1½ lbs Beef tenderloin, cut into 1 inch strips
2 TBS Butter
1¼ C and ⅓ C Beef broth
1 tsp Salt
1 Garlic clove, minced
3 C Mushrooms sliced
1 Onion, chopped
3 TBS Corn starch
1 C Sour cream
4 Servings of cooked rice

In a large skillet, melt the butter over medium-high heat. Cook beef in the butter until brown.

Stir in the 1¼ cup of beef broth, salt, and garlic into the skillet. Heat to boiling, reduce heat, cover and simmer for 10 minutes or until the beef is tender.

Stir in the mushrooms and onions. Cover and simmer for an additional 10 minutes.

Mix the corn starch and ⅓ cup of beef broth in a covered container. Gradually stir this into the beef mixture. Heat to boiling, stirring frequently. Boil for 1 minute then reduce heat to low.

Stir in the sour cream and heat until hot.

Serve over the cooked rice.

Beef Tamales

2 lbs Roast beef
½ tsp Kosher salt
¼ tsp Pepper
2 Onions, sliced
12 Garlic cloves
8 oz New Mexico chilies, tops and seeds removed
1 TBS Caraway seeds
1 TBS Chili powder
3 tsp Kosher salt
3-4 dz Dried corn husks
4 C Minsa® masa
1 TBS Baking powder
4 C Beef broth, warm
1 C Shortening

Set oven to 325°.

Rub the ½ tsp of kosher salt and ¼ tsp of pepper onto all sides of the roast beef. Sear both sides of the roast, in a skillet over medium heat, until it reaches a golden brown. Place the roast in a roasting pan and cover the roast with water. Add 1 sliced onion and 6 garlic cloves. Cook for 2 hours or until meat is tender and easily tears off. When done, transfer the roast to a plate to cool then shred the beef by hand.

Beef Tamales
Continued

Place the chilies in a large stock pot and cover with water. Add the caraway seeds, 1 sliced onion, and 6 garlic cloves. Boil for 20 minutes or until the chilies are soft.

Using tongs, transfer the chilies to a blender along with 1 C of the chili water. Puree until smooth then strain the sauce to remove any chili seeds or skin. Transfer the sauce to a large bowl and stir in the chili powder and 3 tsp of kosher salt. Add all of the shredded beef to the sauce and stir thoroughly. Cover with a damp towel and set aside.

Separate the dried corn husks and remove the silk. Soak them in a sink filled with warm water for 30 minutes. This will loosen the corn husks and make them easier to work with.

In a large bowl, combine the Minsa® masa and 1 TBS of baking powder. Gradually add the warm beef broth, kneading the masa with your fingers. Place 1 C of shortening in a small bowl and beat until fluffy. Mix the shortening with the masa mix until it reaches a spongy like texture. Cover the bowl with a damp towel and set aside.

Drain the corn husks, then rinse and dry each one. Place on a cookie sheet. Place a damp towel over the corn husks and set aside.

Beef Tamales
Continued

Now it's time to roll the tamales. On a large counter or table, set out the corn husks, masa mix, and sauce mix. Place a corn husk on a plate, smooth side up and the narrow end facing you. Spread about ¼ C of the masa mix in the upper to middle left side of the corn husk. Spread about 2-3 TBS of the sauce mix on top of the masa mix. Turn the plate, with the tamale ingredients closest to you and the narrow end facing right. Fold the tamale over once; insert the narrow end of the corn husk, and roll the tamale out, making sure it's tightly rolled. Pinch the top closed. Stand the rolled tamales in a large steamer or colander. Repeat these steps until all of the ingredients are gone.

Place the steamer, full of tamales, in a large pot over 2 inches of low boiling water. Do not let the water touch the tamales. Cover and steam for 2 hours. Check the water levels often to make sure the water doesn't boil out.

The tamales are finished when the inside easily pulls away from the corn husk. The tamale should be soft and firm. Serve with salsa, sour cream, or any other desired topping. You can freeze any remaining tamales to reheat at any time.

Beef Tenderloin with Horseradish Sauce

8 Garlic cloves, minced
1 tsp Salt
2 C Heavy cream
¼ C Horseradish, bottled and drained
¼ tsp Pepper
1 Tenderloin roast, tied
⅓ C Cracked black pepper
2 tsp Water
2 tsp Salt
1 tsp Corn starch
1 tsp Oregano
1 tsp Garlic powder
½ tsp Paprika
2 TBS Olive oil

Set oven to 450°.

In a medium saucepan, simmer the heavy cream for 20 minutes. Transfer to a small bowl.

Add the garlic, salt, pepper and horseradish to the cream and mash until tender. Whip the cream mixture until it reaches a sauce consistency. Refrigerate until needed.

In a medium bowl, stir together the cracked pepper, water, salt, corn starch, oregano, garlic powder, and paprika.

Beef Tenderloin
Continued

Rub the olive oil all over the roast, and then roll the tenderloin in the spices, making sure it's evenly covered.

Place tenderloin in a shallow roasting pan and cook for 10 minutes.

Reduce heat to 425° and cook until the center of the roast reaches at least 130° for medium rare, about 20 to 25 minutes. Cook the tenderloin to your preference.

Remove from oven and let stand for 10 minutes before adding the sauce and carving.

Chicken Fried Steak

4 Cube steaks
¾ C Tapioca flour
¾ C Arrowroot flour
½ tsp Kosher salt
¼ tsp Pepper
1 C Organic shortening
2 Eggs
¼ C Milk

Begin by making the flour mixture. In a large bowl, stir together the tapioca flour, arrowroot flour, kosher salt, and pepper. In a medium size bowl add the eggs and milk together and stir gently.

In a medium to large sized cast iron skillet place the shortening over medium-low heat to melt. Make sure the pan heats evenly.

Once the shortening has melted, you may begin. Dip a steak into the egg batter then into the flour mixture, making sure to evenly coat the steak. Place carefully into skillet, making sure not to splatter the shortening. Repeat this process.

Cook the steaks for 5 minutes then turn. Cook for another 5 minutes then turn again. Lower heat, and then cook the steak for a total of 15 minutes, stirring occasionally.

When the steaks are finished, place on a plate and cover with paper towels. Let cool for 2-4 minutes, and then serve.

Hobo Dinner

1 pkg Whole button mushrooms
2 Zucchini, sliced
2 Squash, sliced
2 Onions, ringed
4 Carrot stalks, sliced
8 Yukon gold potatoes, cubed
2 lbs Beef stew meat

For each packet you will need:
1 Garlic clove
4 TBS Worcestershire sauce
½ tsp Celery salt
½ tsp Garlic salt
1 tsp Kosher salt
Pepper to taste

Prepare all of the vegetables as shown above and separate into small bowls.

In a large mixing bowl, add a handful of mushrooms, zucchini, squash, onions, carrots, potatoes, and the raw stew meat. Next, add the garlic clove, Worcestershire sauce, celery salt, garlic salt, kosher salt, and pepper. Stir thoroughly until everything is evenly coated. Place the entire contents of the bowl onto a large piece of foil, large enough to wrap all ingredients with foil. Several pieces of foil may be needed to assure there is no leaking during the grilling process.

Repeat this process until you have the desired amount of packets. Cook on grill for 45 minutes.

Remove from the grill, place the packet onto a plate, slice open the packet, and serve immediately.

Lemon Rosemary Pork Tenderloin

6 TBS Extra virgin olive oil
1 C Fresh lemon juice
⅓ C Fresh rosemary, chopped
¼ C Fresh parsley, chopped
1 TBS Crushed red pepper
5 Garlic cloves, chopped
2 Pork tenderloins, about ¾ lb each
Salt and pepper to taste

In a large resealable bag, mix the olive oil, lemon juice, rosemary, parsley, red pepper, and garlic. Mix well.

Add the pork tenderloins to the bag. Marinade the tenderloins for 2-4 hours.

Set oven to 400°.

Heat a large skillet over medium heat.

Remove the tenderloins from the bag and scrape off the rosemary and parsley. Season with salt and pepper.

Place the tenderloins in the skillet, searing all sides until browned, for about 5 minutes.

Transfer the tenderloins to a large baking sheet and cook for 15 minutes or until the center reaches 130°.

Cover the tenderloins with foil and cook for an additional 5 minutes. Remove from oven and let stand for 10 minutes before carving.

Serve immediately.

Pineapple Ginger Ribs

1 Rack of ribs
Salt and pepper to taste
3 Garlic cloves, minced
1 C Pineapple, crushed
¼ tsp Ginger, grated
¼ C Norlander's Original® Mesquite sauce
½ C Water

Set oven to 275°.

Place the ribs in a large baking dish. Rub the salt and pepper all over the ribs. Cook for 45 minutes.

Combine the remaining ingredients in a food processor and mix until well blended.

Transfer to a small bowl.

Remove the ribs and, using a basting brush, spread the pineapple ginger sauce all over the ribs. Make sure the ribs are evenly coated with the sauce. Reserve a small amount to apply after cooking.

Cook for an additional 15 minutes.

Remove the ribs and apply the reserved sauce. Let the ribs cool for 10 minutes before cutting.

Pineapple Glazed Ham

6 lb Fully cooked, smoked, bone-in ham
1 C Brown sugar, packed
1 TBS Cornstarch
½ tsp Salt
1 can Crushed pineapples, un-drained
Juice of 1 lime

Set oven to 325°.

Place the ham in a shallow roasting pan and cook, uncovered, for 1 hour.

In a medium pan, mix together the brown sugar, corn starch, and salt. Stir in the pineapples and lime juice. Stirring constantly, bring the glaze to a boil. Remove from heat.

Remove the ham and apply the pineapple glaze. Using a basting brush, make sure the ham gets evenly coated with the glaze.

Cook for an additional 30 minutes.

When the ham is finished, remove from oven, cover with foil, and let stand 10 minutes before carving.

Pot Roast

1½ to 2 lbs. Beef arm roast
3 tsp Kosher salt
1 tsp Garlic powder
1 tsp Onion powder
4-5 Potatoes, cubed
1 Onion, sliced
1½ C Baby carrots
1 C Celery, chopped
1 C Mushrooms, sliced
5 Garlic cloves, minced

Set the oven to 300°.

Rub the salt, garlic powder, and onion powder over the entire roast. Set the roast in a roasting pan, cover, and cook for 2 hours.

Prepare all vegetables.

When the roast has cooked for 2 hours, remove and add the remaining ingredients. Cover.

Cook for an additional 2 hours or until all vegetables are tender.

Serve immediately.

Pulled Pork

1 Pork shoulder roast
2 Onions, sliced
2 C Water
1 bottle Gluten free BBQ sauce
1 Onion, chopped

Place 1 sliced onion on the bottom of a crock pot. Add the roast and the water. Cook on low for 8 hours or on high for 4 hours.

Drain the liquid and remove the pork roast. Cut all excess fat from the roast. Chop the meat coarsely and return to the crock pot.

Add the bar-b-que sauce and the chopped onions to the crock pot and cook, on low, for an additional 4-6 hours. Stir occasionally.

Roasted Pork Tenderloin

1 TBS Olive oil
1 tsp Salt
½ tsp Pepper
1 tsp Oregano
1 tsp Basil
2 Garlic cloves, crushed
2 Pork Tenderloins, about ¾ lb each

Set oven to 450°.

Grease a shallow roasting pan with cooking spray.

Mix all ingredients together, except the pork tenderloins, until the mixture makes a thick paste. Rub the paste on the pork tenderloins.

Cook, uncovered, for 30 minutes.

Remove from oven, cover with foil, and let stand for 15 minutes until serving.

Shepherd's Pie

2 Packages ground turkey meat
1 Onion, chopped
2 Garlic cloves, minced
4 Large potatoes, cubed
1 Can green beans, drained
1 Can diced tomatoes
2 Cans corn, drained
1 Can stewed tomatoes
2 C Sliced mushrooms
½ tsp Garlic salt
½ tsp Kosher salt
3 TBS Butter
Dash of pepper

Set oven to 350 degrees.

Brown the ground turkey with the chopped onion and the minced garlic.

While the meat is cooking, place 3 cups of water into a large pot. Bring to a boil and add the cubed potatoes. Cook until tender.

In a large mixing bowl, combine 1 can of drained green beans, 1 can of diced tomatoes, 2 cans of drained corn, 1 can of stewed tomatoes, 2 cups mushrooms, ½ tsp garlic salt, ½ tsp kosher salt, and pepper to your liking. Stir until mixed thoroughly.

Shepherd's Pie
Continued

When the ground turkey is finished, add it to the mixing bowl, holding the vegetables, and stir well.

Place into a 9x13 casserole dish. Level the top of the casserole.

When the potatoes are tender, drain and place them into a mixing bowl. Add ½ tsp garlic salt, 3 TBS of butter, and pepper to taste and mix. Place mashed potato layer on the top of the casserole. Smooth the potatoes, making the top surface flat.

Bake at 350 degrees for 30 minutes.

Serve immediately.

Slow Cooked Pork Ribs

1 Rack of ribs
1 tsp Garlic salt
1 tsp Onion powder
3 TBS Brown sugar
2 TBS and ¼ C Honey
1 C Gluten Free BBQ Sauce
Salt & Pepper to taste

Set oven to 200°.

Place the ribs in a large baking dish. Using clean hands, rub the salt, pepper, onion powder, garlic salt, and brown sugar into the ribs. Bake for 15 minutes.

Remove the ribs from the oven and add 2 TBS of honey, making sure to coat all of the ribs.

Set oven to 275° and bake for an additional 30 minutes.

Remove the ribs from the oven and drizzle the ¼ C honey over ribs, making sure to evenly coat the ribs.

Bake for an additional 30 minutes.

Remove the ribs and drizzle the BBQ sauce onto the ribs. Bake for an additional 15 minutes.

Serve immediately.

Southwest Pork Chops with Corn Salsa

4 Pork chops
1 tsp Cumin
1 tsp Chili powder
1 tsp Garlic powder
1 tsp Onion powder
1 can Sweet corn, drained
1 can Black beans, drained
1 can Diced tomatoes, drained
1 Garlic clove, minced
Salt & pepper to taste

Combine the cumin, chili powder, garlic powder, and onion powder together in a small bowl. Rub onto each pork chop.

In a large skillet, over medium heat, cook the pork chops for 15 to 20 minutes.

Meanwhile, in a medium bowl, combine the corn, black beans, and diced tomatoes. Mix well. Stir in the garlic, salt, and pepper.

Transfer the pork chops to a serving plate. Pour ⅓ cup of the corn salsa onto the pork chops and serve immediately.

Taco Meat

2 Packages ground beef
1 TBS Onion salt
1 tsp Garlic salt
2 tsp Paprika
1 ½ tsp Chili powder
½ C Water

Brown ground beef on medium heat.

Add the onion salt, garlic salt, paprika, and chili powder and stir. Add water. Stir. Bring to a boil, lower heat to medium low, and let simmer for 10 minutes.

Serve taco meat in tacos, taco salad, or anything else you would like to use taco seasoned meat.

Taco Wrap

1 Package ground beef
1 TBS Onion salt
1 tsp Garlic salt
2 tsp Paprika
1½ tsp Chili powder
½ C Water
Corn tortillas
Taco shells
1 Can Refried beans

Brown ground beef on medium heat.

Add the onion salt, garlic salt, paprika, and chili powder and stir. Add water. Stir. Bring to a boil, lower heat to medium low, and let simmer for 10 minutes.

Heat the refried beans then place a heaping spoonful onto a corn tortilla. Place a taco shell in the middle of the corn tortilla then wrap the tortilla around the shell.

Fill the taco with the taco meat and any other desired taco toppings.

Serve immediately.

Poultry: Chicken & Turkey

Baked Honey Lime Chicken Legs

Chicken Cacciatore

Chicken Stir Fry

Chicken Teriyaki Legs

Citrus Chicken

Crunchy Garlic Chicken

Fried Chicken

Hawaiian Chicken

Lemon Basil Chicken

Orange Chicken

Roasted Chicken

Smothered Chicken

Spicy Chicken Enchiladas

Turkey and Feta Cheese Pizza

Turkey Meatloaf

Baked Honey Lime Chicken Legs

12 Chicken legs, skin removed
2 TBS Butter
1 TBS Vegetable oil
1 TBS Lime zest
Juice of 1 lime
2 Limes, wedged for garnish
⅓ C Honey
4 Garlic cloves, minced
1 tsp Kosher salt
2 TBS Parsley

Set oven to 450°.

Melt the butter in a 9x13 casserole dish. In a large bowl, combine the lime zest, lime juice, honey, garlic, and salt. Stir well.

Arrange the chicken legs in the casserole dish. Drizzle the marinade on the chicken. Toss to assure even coating. Cook for 35-40 minutes. Occasionally, brush the chicken, using a basting brush, with the juices in the pan.

When the chicken is finished, transfer to a serving plate and drizzle the excess sauce onto the chicken.

Sprinkle the parsley on the chicken and garnish with the lime wedges. Serve immediately.

Chicken Cacciatore

3 lbs Cut up broiler-fryer chicken
½ C Arrowroot
¼ C Vegetable oil
1 Bell pepper, cut into strips
2 Onions, sliced
1 can Diced tomatoes
1 can Tomato sauce
1 C Mushrooms, sliced
½ tsp Oregano
¼ tsp Basil
1 tsp Salt
3 Garlic cloves, minced

Coat the chicken with the arrowroot.

Heat oil in a large skillet over medium heat. Cook chicken in oil for 20 minutes or until brown on all sides then drain.

Stir in the bell pepper, onions, diced tomatoes, tomato sauce, mushrooms, oregano, basil, salt, and garlic with the chicken. Heat to boiling then reduce heat, cover and simmer for 30 minutes or until juice of chicken is no longer pink.

Serve immediately.

Chicken Stir Fry

4 Chicken tenderloins, thawed
½ Bag of frozen stir fry vegetables
½ Bag of pepper stir fry mix
1 C Portobello mushrooms, sliced
2 C Rice, cooked
1 TBS Olive oil
1 tsp Garlic salt
Salt and Pepper to taste

Set oven to 425 degrees.

Cook chicken until the center temperature reaches 165 degrees.

Prepare the rice according to the packages directions.

In a large pan or wok, add the olive oil, frozen stir fry vegetables, pepper stir fry mix, and mushrooms. Set stove to medium low. Simmer the vegetables over medium to low heat while the chicken is cooking.

When the chicken is cooked, cut it into 1 inch pieces. Add the chicken, garlic salt, and salt and pepper to the vegetable mix and stir.

Serve over rice.

Chicken Teriyaki Legs

14 Chicken legs
¼ C Tapioca flour
¾ C Arrowroot
1 tsp Kosher salt
½ tsp Pepper
2 TBS Butter
½ C and ⅓ C Norlander's Original® Mesquite Sauce
1 C Water

Set oven to 350°.

Melt the butter in a 9x13 casserole dish.

Place the tapioca flour, arrowroot, salt, and pepper into a large zip lock bag and mix well. Add the legs, 2-3 at a time, to the flour mixture. Make sure each leg is evenly coated and place into the casserole dish. Bake for 25 minutes.

In a large bowl mix together ½ cup of Norlander's Original® Mesquite Sauce and water; set aside.

Remove the chicken and turn each of the legs. Cook for an additional 25 minutes.

When chicken has cooked for 50 minutes, remove the chicken legs and pour the sauce over the legs. A basting brush will help to evenly coat the legs. Cook for 10 minutes, turning once.

Chicken Teriyaki Legs
Continued

Pour ⅓ cup Norlander's Original® Mesquite Sauce concentrate into a bowl.

Remove the chicken from the oven.

Using the basting brush, spread the concentrate onto the chicken legs and cook for 5 minutes, turn legs, and cook for an additional 5 minutes.

Serve immediately.

Citrus Chicken

6 Chicken breasts, skinless and boneless
½ C Frozen (thawed) orange juice concentrate
¼ C Olive oil
⅓ C Lemon juice, fresh
2 TBS Orange zest
1 tsp Salt
2 Garlic cloves, minced

In a large bowl, mix all ingredients except for the chicken. Stir well.

Place the chicken in a large casserole dish. Pour the citrus marinade over the chicken, turning once to evenly coat the chicken. Cover and refrigerate at least 2 hours before cooking.

Turn on the grill to medium heat.

Remove the chicken from the casserole dish. Set the marinade aside to use again. Pour the marinade into a small bowl to use later.

Place the chicken on the grill for 20 minutes, turning occasionally and brushing with marinade. Cook until the juices no longer run pink or the center reaches 165°.

Heat the remaining marinade to a boil in a small saucepan. Pour over the chicken and serve immediately.

Crunchy Garlic Chicken

6 Chicken breasts, boneless and skinless
2 TBS Butter
2 TBS Milk
1 TBS Parsley
1 tsp Salt
½ tsp Garlic powder
2 C Lays potato chips, crushed
3 TBS Fresh parsley, chopped
½ tsp Paprika
2 TBS Butter, melted

Set oven to 425°.

Grease a 13x9 casserole dish.

In a large bowl, mix 2 tablespoons of butter, the milk, 1 tablespoon of parsley, salt, and garlic powder. In a separate bowl, mix the Lays potato chips, fresh parsley, and paprika.

Dip the chicken into the liquid mixture, and then dip it into the batter mixture. Make sure each chicken is coated thoroughly with the Lays mixture. Place the chicken in the pan. Drizzle the melted butter over all of the dipped chicken breasts.

Cook for 25 minutes, or until the center reaches 165°. Serve immediately.

Fried Chicken

1 pkg Chicken thighs, legs, or breasts
¾ C Tapioca flour
¾ C Arrowroot flour
½ tsp Kosher salt
¼ tsp Pepper
1 C Organic shortening
2 Eggs
¼ C Milk

Begin by making the flour mixture. In a large bowl, stir together the tapioca flour, arrowroot flour, kosher salt, and pepper.

In a medium size bowl add the eggs and milk together and stir gently.

In a medium to large sized cast iron skillet place the shortening over medium-low heat to melt. Make sure the pan heats evenly. Rinse the chicken in cool water and set aside on a plate.

Once the shortening has melted, you may begin. Dip a piece of chicken into the egg batter then into the flour mixture, making sure to evenly coat the chicken. Place carefully into skillet, making sure not to splatter the shortening. Repeat this process. Only cook 3 pieces of chicken at a time, to ensure the chicken is cooked evenly.

Fried Chicken
Continued

Cook the chicken for 5 minutes then turn. Cook for another 5 minutes then turn again. Lower heat to medium-low. Cook the chicken for 25 minutes, turning every 4 minutes. When the center of the chicken has reached 165°, remove the chicken from the skillet, place on a plate, and cover with paper towels.

Let the fried chicken cool for 2-4 minutes, and then serve.

Hawaiian Chicken

4-6 Chicken breasts
2 C Pineapple juice
3 TBS Worcestershire sauce
⅓ C Soy sauce
2 TBS Brown sugar
1 can Pineapples, sliced

Pierce each chicken breast.

In a resealable bag, add the pineapple juice, Worcestershire sauce, soy sauce, and brown sugar. Mix well.

Add the chicken to the bag, place in the refrigerator, and let marinate for 4-6 hours.

Transfer chicken to a preheated grill and cook until the center reaches 165°. Discard the marinade.

Garnish the Hawaiian chicken with the pineapple slices and serve immediately.

Lemon Basil Chicken

2 Chicken breasts; thawed
6 Lemon wedges
1 Tsp Basil
4 Tsp Balsamic vinegar
3 Tsp Olive oil

Set oven to 400°

Mix lemon wedges, basil, balsamic vinegar, and olive oil together in a large zip lock bag. Mix well. Place chicken breasts into bag and let marinade for 10-15 minutes.

Place chicken into a small baking dish and cook for 40 minutes.

Serve immediately.

Orange Chicken

2 lbs Chicken breasts, cut into 1 inch pieces
1 Egg
2 tsp Salt
Vegetable oil, for frying
½ C Cornstarch
¼ C Sorghum
1 TBS Gingerroot, minced
1 Garlic clove, minced
¾ tsp Chili pepper
1 tsp Vinegar
¼ C Water
2 tsp Soy sauce
2 tsp Water
5 TBS Sugar
5 TBS Vinegar
Zest of 1 orange
Juice of 1 orange
¼ C Scallions, finely chopped
1 TBS Sesame seeds

Heat about 1 inch of vegetable oil in a large skillet over medium heat.

In a small bowl, mix together the egg and salt.

In a separate bowl, add the cornstarch and sorghum.

Dip the chicken pieces into the egg mixture then into the flour mixture. Place the chicken in the skillet and cook until the chicken browns on all sides.

Add the gingerroot, garlic, chili pepper, vinegar and water to the skillet. Bring to a slight boil, reduce heat, and simmer for 5 minutes.

Meanwhile, in a small bowl, combine the soy sauce, water, sugar, vinegar, orange zest, and orange juice. Mix well.

Pour the orange sauce over the chicken and simmer for an additional 10 minutes.

When the chicken is done, transfer to a serving plate. Garnish with sesame seeds and scallions.

Roasted Chicken

1 Whole chicken
½ Stick butter, melted
1 tsp Garlic salt
½ tsp Parsley
½ tsp Onion powder
¼ tsp Kosher salt

Set oven to 325°.

In a small bowl, mix together the melted butter, garlic salt, parsley, onion powder, and kosher salt.

Using a meat injector, inject the buttery mixture into the fatty parts of the chicken. Drizzle any remaining butter mixture over the chicken.

Place the chicken in a large casserole dish and cook, covered, for 3 hours.

Serve immediately

Smothered Chicken

4 Chicken breasts, boneless and skinless
1 tsp Oregano
1 tsp Salt
½ tsp Pepper
1 tsp Garlic powder
¼ tsp Cayenne pepper
2 TBS Butter
1 Bell pepper, thinly sliced
1 Onion, thinly sliced
1 C Mushrooms, sliced
½ C Mozzarella cheese, shredded
¼ C Parmesan cheese

Heat a large skillet over medium heat. Spray with cooking spray.

In a small bowl, mix together the oregano, salt, garlic powder, pepper, and cayenne pepper. Sprinkle both sides of the chicken with the spice mixture. Cook the chicken in the skillet for 8-10 minutes on each side, turning once, until juice is no longer pink. Remove chicken from skillet and keep warm.

Melt the butter in the same skillet over medium heat. Cook the bell pepper and onion in the butter for 5 minutes, stirring occasionally. Stir in the mushrooms, and cook for an additional 5 minutes, or until vegetables are tender.

Place the chicken in the skillet and place the vegetables on top of the chicken. Sprinkle the cheeses on top; remove from heat, and cover. Let stand until cheese is melted.

Serve immediately.

Spicy Chicken Enchiladas

3 TBS Olive oil
10 Gluten Free Corn tortillas
4 Chicken breasts
1 Medium onion
¼ C Fresh cilantro
1 Anaheim pepper
1 can Gluten Free Mexican rice
2 C Cheddar cheese
1 C Monterrey jack cheese
2 C Sour cream
Sauce:
1 can Green chilies
2 C La Botanera hot sauce

Set oven to 425°.

Bake the chicken until the center reaches 165°, about 35 minutes.

In a large skillet, over medium heat, add the olive oil. Place 1 corn tortilla at a time into the skillet, lightly frying each side for 10-15 seconds. Place on a plate and set aside.

Chop the onion, cilantro, and pepper in a chopper and set aside. Add the Mexican rice to a bowl and set aside. Also, place the cheese in a small bowl and set aside.

When the chicken is finished, gently tear the chicken apart, shredding it into small pieces. Place in small bowl and set aside. Set oven to 350°.

In a medium mixing bowl, add the green chilies and La Botanera hot sauce and stir.

Place a corn tortilla on a plate and add the chicken, onion mixture, rice, and cheese. Gently roll the tortilla, full of ingredients, and place seam side down into a 9x13 casserole dish. Repeat steps with the remaining ingredients.

When the casserole dish is full, pour the sauce over the enchiladas and distribute evenly.

Cook for 25 minutes.

When the timer goes off, spread the sour cream evenly over the enchiladas and sprinkle the Monterrey jack cheese on top.

Cook an additional 5-7 minutes, or until cheese is melted. Serve immediately.

Turkey and Feta Cheese Pizza

1 lb Ground turkey meat
1 Garlic clove, minced
½ C Feta cheese
½ C Pesto
1 Bell pepper, thinly sliced
1 Onion, thinly sliced
½ C Artichoke hearts
4 Gluten free personal size pizza crusts

In a large skillet, brown the ground turkey with the garlic.

Spread the pesto all over the tops of the crusts.

Add the bell peppers, onions, and artichoke hearts. Sprinkle the ground turkey and feta cheese over the pizzas.

Cook according to the directions of the pizza crust.

Serve immediately.

Turkey Meatloaf

1 lb Ground turkey meat, raw
1 Egg
1 TBS Worcestershire sauce
½ Onion, chopped
½ Green pepper, chopped
1 tsp Celery salt
1 tsp Garlic salt
1 tsp Onion salt
½ C V-8 juice

Topping:
½ C Ketchup
2 TBS Worcestershire sauce

Set oven to 375° degrees.

Place raw turkey meat and egg in a large bowl. Stir, and then add the Worcestershire sauce, onion, green pepper, celery salt, garlic salt, onion powder, and V-8 juice to the meat. Mix thoroughly.

Cook for 50 minutes at 375 degrees.

Thoroughly mix the topping ingredients together.

When the timer goes off, remove the meatloaf and add the topping. Cook for an additional 10 minutes, remove, and serve immediately.

RICE & PASTA

Baked Ziti

Cheesy Lasagna

Chicken Casserole

Chicken & Rice

Chicken Fried Rice

Chicken Spaghetti

Chili Cheese Macaroni

College Noodles

Green Tea Chicken & Rice

Macaroni & Cheese

Onion Rice

Pasta Primavera

Red Beans & Rice

Spanish Rice

Spinach and Artichoke Pasta

Baked Ziti

1 lb Ground turkey meat
1 tsp Italian seasoning
1 pkg Gluten free pasta (not spaghetti noodles)
1 Egg
2 C Shredded mozzarella cheese
1 C Ricotta cheese
1 can Italian spaghetti sauce
1 C Shredded parmesan cheese

Set oven to 350°.

Brown the ground turkey with the Italian seasoning. Cook the pasta according to the packages directions.

In a large bowl, combine the egg, mozzarella cheese, and ricotta cheese. Stir well. Then add the spaghetti sauce to the cheese mix.

Drain pasta and transfer to the large bowl. Add the ground turkey and stir until it is evenly mixed.

Transfer the ziti to a 9x13 casserole dish, distributing it evenly.

Sprinkle the parmesan cheese evenly across the top. Bake for 20 minutes. Serve immediately.

Cheesy Lasagna

1 lb Ground beef
2 Garlic cloves, minced
1 box Gluten free lasagna
1 jar Gluten free spaghetti sauce
½ tsp Basil
½ tsp Oregano
1 Egg
15 oz Ricotta cheese
2 C Mozzarella cheese
Parmesan cheese

Set oven to 350°.

Cook pasta according to package instructions.

In a large skillet, brown the ground beef with the garlic, basil, and oregano.

Add spaghetti sauce to the browned meat and stir.

In a medium bowl, mix together the egg, ricotta cheese, and mozzarella cheese. Stir in the ground beef. Mix well.

In a 9x13 baking dish, place a layer of lasagna on the bottom, then put a layer of the mix. End with the sauce as the top layer. Top with parmesan cheese.

Bake for 30 minutes covered. Remove foil and cook, uncovered, for an additional 10 minutes.

Chicken Casserole

1½ C Chicken, cooked and shredded
1 C Mushrooms, sliced
1 can Peas, drained
½ Onion, chopped
1 Scallion, chopped
1 can Diced tomatoes, drained
2 Garlic cloves, chopped
Salt to taste
1 pkg Gluten free pasta
1 C Cheddar cheese, shredded

Cook pasta according to the packages directions, but replace the water with chicken broth.

Set oven to 350°.

In a large bowl, combine the chicken, mushrooms, peas, onion, scallion, diced tomatoes, and garlic. Mix well.

Add cooked pasta. Mix well.

Transfer to a 9x13 casserole dish and spread evenly.

Cook for 20 minutes.

Remove from oven and sprinkle the cheese on top of the casserole. Cook for an additional 5 minutes or until the cheese is bubbly. Serve immediately

Chicken & Rice

1 Chicken breast, cooked and cut into 1 inch strips
2 C Rice
1 C Chicken broth
1 C Water
½ Onion, diced
1 Can sliced mushrooms
2 TBS Butter
½ tsp Garlic, minced

Set oven to 425°.

Cook chicken until the center reaches 165°. Cut into 1 inch strips.

In a large sauce pan, sauté the onion, mushrooms, and garlic with the butter. Add the water, chicken broth, and rice to the sauce pan and cook until rice is tender.

Stir in mushrooms and chicken. Serve immediately.

Chicken Fried Rice

4 C Cooked Rice
2 Chicken breasts, cooked
1 Egg
3 TBS Butter
½ C Frozen peas and carrots
1 tsp Kosher salt
½ Medium onion, chopped
¼ C Soy Sauce

Set oven to 425°. Cook chicken until the center reaches 165°.

Cook the rice according to the package directions.

Place a large wok or skillet over medium heat. Crack the egg into the wok and stir constantly. Next add the butter and the frozen peas and carrots. Stir until mixed together. Place all of the rice into the wok and continue to stir. Add the salt, onion, and soy sauce. Stir. Lower heat to medium-low.

Cut the cooked chicken into ½ strips then add to the fried rice.

Stir and cook for an additional 10 minutes. Serve immediately.

Chicken Spaghetti

1 pkg Gluten free spaghetti
7 Chicken tenderloins, cooked & cut into 1 inch strips
1 pkg Whole button mushrooms
1 Bell pepper, chopped
1 Onion, chopped
1 Can Gluten free cream of mushroom soup
½ C Gluten free bread crumbs
1 C Chicken broth
1 C Shredded parmesan cheese
½ tsp Garlic salt
Salt and pepper to taste

Cook the spaghetti according to the packages directions.

Set oven to 300°.

In a large bowl mix the onions, mushrooms, and bell pepper together. Stir in the cream of mushroom soup, garlic salt, and the bread crumbs.

Drain the spaghetti then add to the vegetables. Stir in the chicken and the chicken broth.

Place the chicken spaghetti into the casserole dish. Sprinkle the cheese over the top of the spaghetti and cook for 30 minutes.

Serve immediately.

Chili Cheese Macaroni

1 C Uncooked gluten free elbow macaroni
1 lb Lean ground beef
1 Onion, chopped
3 Garlic cloves, minced
1 can Kidney beans, drained
1 can Diced tomatoes, un-drained
1 can Tomato sauce
1 can Tomato paste
1 TBS Chili powder
1 tsp Cumin
1 C Sharp cheddar cheese, shredded

Cook the elbow macaroni according to packages directions.

While the macaroni is cooking, brown the beef, onion, and garlic together in a large pan, stirring occasionally.

Drain the macaroni. Add the macaroni to the ground beef along with the kidney beans, diced tomatoes, tomato sauce, tomato paste, chili powder, and cumin. Heat to boiling, stirring occasionally. Reduce heat and simmer, uncovered, for 20 minutes, stirring occasionally.

Sprinkle with cheese and serve immediately.

College Noodles

1 Pkg Gluten Free pasta
1 Can Whole peeled tomatoes, drained
1 Can Diced Tomatoes, drained
2 tsp Garlic salt
1 tsp Onion powder
¼ tsp Kosher salt

Cook the pasta according to the packages directions.

Drain the pasta and return to pan. Add the whole tomatoes and the diced tomatoes. Stir occasionally, over medium heat, until the tomatoes are hot. Stir in the garlic salt, onion powder, and kosher salt.

Serve immediately.

Green-Tea Chicken & Rice

2 Chicken breasts, cooked and cubed
2 TBS Olive oil
1 Onion, chopped
1 tsp. Garlic salt
1 Green-tea bag
1 C Uncooked rice
2 C Water
Salt & Pepper to taste

In a large skillet, over medium heat, sauté the olive oil, cooked chicken, and half of the onions. Stir in the garlic salt, salt, and pepper. Cook for 10 -15 minutes.

Add the remaining onions, water, rice, and green-tea bag to the skillet. Stir well. Simmer for 15 minutes, stirring occasionally.

Reduce heat, cover, and simmer for an additional 10 minutes, or until rice is fully cooked. Serve immediately.

Macaroni & Cheese

1 pkg Gluten Free elbow pasta
⅓ C Milk
3 TBS Butter
4 oz Velveeta cheese

Cook pasta, following the directions given.

When pasta is finished, drain, return pot to stove, and put on medium heat. Add the milk, butter, and cheese. Stir. Add the drained pasta to the cheese mixture and stir until the cheese is melted. Serve immediately.

Onion Rice

1 TBS Butter
1 Small onion, chopped
¾ C Rice
1 C Chicken broth

Sautee the onions and butter in a medium sauce pan.

When onions are caramelized, add the chicken broth and rice.

Stir well. Cook until rice is tender.

Pasta Primavera

1 pkg Uncooked gluten free fettuccine or linguine
1 TBS Olive oil
1 C Broccoli
1 C Cauliflower
2 Carrots, thinly sliced
1 C Frozen green peas
1 Onion, chopped
½ C Mushrooms sliced
1 jar Classico Mushroom Alfredo Sauce
¼ C Parmesan cheese
1 tsp Salt
¼ tsp Pepper

Cook the fettuccine according to the packages directions.

While the pasta is cooking, heat the olive oil in a large skillet over medium heat. Add the broccoli, cauliflower, carrots, peas, onion, and mushrooms. Cook for 6-8 minutes, stirring frequently. Remove from heat and cover to keep warm.

Add the Classico Mushroom Alfredo Sauce to the vegetable mixture. Stir well.

Drain the pasta. Stir the fettuccine into the sauce mixture and heat thoroughly.

Sprinkle with parmesan cheese and serve immediately.

Red Beans & Rice

1 lb. Red kidney beans
12 oz. Sausage
1 tsp Basil
1 tsp Oregano
1 tsp Paprika
1 tsp Thyme
1 tsp Cayenne pepper
1 TBS Salt
⅛ tsp Bay leaves
4 C Beef broth
1 Garlic clove, minced
1 C Rice

Put the kidney beans in a large pot with 3 inches of water covering the beans. Let sit for 1 hour.

Mix together the basil, oregano, paprika, thyme, cayenne pepper, salt, and bay leaves in a small bowl and set aside.

Drain the beans from the pot. Return beans to pot and add the beef broth. Add the spice mixture and garlic; stir well. Bring to a boil, reduce heat, and cover. Cook until the beans are tender, about 2 hours, stirring occasionally. Make sure the liquid doesn't evaporate from the beans throughout the cooking process.

Brown the sausage in a medium skillet.

After the beans have softened, add the sausage to the beans. Add the rice and stir thoroughly. Cook for about 45 minutes, or until the rice is tender.

Serve immediately.

Spanish Rice

2 TBS Olive oil
1 C Uncooked white long-grain rice
1 Onion, finely chopped
2½ C Water
2 tsp Salt
¾ tsp Chili powder
¼ tsp Garlic powder
1 Bell pepper, finely chopped
1 can Tomato sauce
1 can Green chilies

Heat the oil in a large skillet over medium heat. Cook the rice and the onion for 5 minutes, stirring frequently, until the rice is golden brown.

Stir in all of the remaining ingredients. Bring to a boil, then reduce heat, and cover. Simmer for 30 minutes, stirring occasionally, or until rice is tender.

Spinach and Artichoke Pasta

8 oz Gluten free short pasta
1 can Artichoke hearts, rinsed and quartered
1 pkg Frozen spinach, thawed
½ C Parmesan cheese, grated
2 C Mozzarella cheese, shredded
Salt and Pepper to taste

Set oven to broil.

Cook the pasta according to the packages directions. Drain and return to the pot.

Add artichoke hearts, spinach, Parmesan cheese, 1 cup of the mozzarella cheese, and salt and pepper. Mix all ingredients well.

Transfer the pasta mixture to an 8x8 casserole dish. Sprinkle the remaining mozzarella cheese on top of the pasta.

Broil until the cheese browns; about 4-5 minutes.

Serve immediately.

SALADS, SALAD DRESSINGS, & SAUCES

Chicken Caesar Salad

Classic Spaghetti Sauce

Cranberry Sauce

Cucumber Pineapple Salsa

Cucumber Salad

Fruit Salad

Honey Bar-B-Que Sauce

Kiwi Salsa

Lemon Vinaigrette

Macaroni Salad

Oregon Potato Salad

Raspberry Vinaigrette

Roasted Garlic Dipping Sauce

Strawberry Vinaigrette

Taco Salad

Waldorf Salad

Chicken Caesar Salad

1 pkg Romaine lettuce
1 chicken breast, cooked and cut into 1 in. strips
½ C Parmesan cheese
Gluten free Caesar salad dressing to taste
1 C Gluten free croutons

Mix all ingredients together in a large bowl.

Serve immediately.

Classic Spaghetti Sauce

1 lb. Ground beef
1 Onion, chopped
4 Garlic cloves, minced
1 28oz can Diced tomatoes
1 12 oz can Tomato paste
1 15 oz can Tomato sauce
8 whole Cherry tomatoes
2 tsp Oregano
½ tsp Italian seasoning
2 tsp Garlic salt
1 C Baby Portobello mushrooms

In a large skillet, brown the meat with the onions and the garlic.

In a large pot, add the diced tomatoes, tomato paste, tomato sauce, and whole tomatoes. Stir well, and then add the oregano and Italian seasoning. Simmer over low heat.

Add the ground beef to the sauce along with the mushrooms and the garlic salt. Simmer on low/medium heat for 30 minutes, stirring occasionally. Serve over your choice of gluten free pasta.

Cranberry Sauce

4 C Fresh cranberries
2 C Sugar
2 C Water
1 TBS Orange zest
1 tsp Cinnamon

Wash cranberries; remove all stems and blemished berries.

In a medium sauce pan, bring the water and sugar to a boil. Boil for 5 minutes.

Stir in the cranberries. Bring to a boil. Boil for an additional 5 minutes or until cranberries pop. Stir in orange zest and cinnamon.

Transfer to a small bowl, cover, and refrigerate at least 3 hours before serving.

Cucumber Pineapple Salsa

1 Cucumber, peeled, sliced, & cubed
½ C Extra virgin olive oil
2 tsp Salt
1 tsp Fresh mint, chopped
½ C Scallions, chopped
2 Garlic cloves, minced
1 tsp Fresh grated ginger
2½ TBS Fresh cilantro, chopped
Juice of 1 lime
1 Yellow azteca pepper, finely chopped
1 C Chopped pineapple
½ tsp Pepper

Mix all ingredients together in a medium bowl.

Refrigerate at least 1 hour before serving.

Serve over any cooked fish.

Cucumber Salad

2 Cucumbers, thinly sliced
3 Tomatoes, wedged
1 Onion, sliced
⅓ C White vinegar
⅓ C Water
1 TBS Sugar
1 tsp Salt
¼ tsp Pepper
¼ tsp Dill

Place the cucumbers, tomatoes, and onion in a medium bowl.

In a Tupperware container, add the vinegar, water, sugar, salt, and pepper. Cover and shake until thoroughly mixed. Pour the sauce over the cucumber mixture. Cover and refrigerate at least 3 hours before serving.

Before serving, sprinkle the dill over the salad.

Fruit Salad

1 can Pitted cherries, drained
2 cans Pineapple chunks, drained
2 C Strawberries, sliced
2 TBS Pineapple juice
3 Oranges, wedged
2 Eggs, beaten
2 TBS Sugar
2 TBS Lemon juice
1 TBS Butter
¾ C Heavy whipping cream

In a medium saucepan, heat the eggs, sugar, lemon juice, pineapple juice, and butter to a boil, stirring constantly. Let cool.

Beat the whipping cream in a chilled bowl until stiff.

Fold the egg mixture into the whipping cream.

Fold in the cherries, pineapples, strawberries, and oranges to the whipping cream mixture and mix well.

Cover and refrigerate at least 12 hours before serving.

Honey Bar-B-Que Sauce

1 C Gluten free BBQ sauce
¼ C Worcestershire sauce
¼ C Honey
½ tsp Garlic salt

Mix all of the above ingredients together in a bowl and stir well.

Serve on pork chops, chicken, etc.

Kiwi Salsa

6 Kiwi, peeled and diced
2 TBS Red onion, minced
½ tsp Chili powder
2 TBS Fresh cilantro, finely chopped
2 tsp Lime zest
2 TBS Lime juice
1 tsp Salt

In a medium bowl, mix the kiwi, red onion, chili powder, cilantro, lime zest, lime juice, and salt together. Add more lime juice or salt to taste.

Serve over ginger salmon or any other type of fish.

Lemon Vinaigrette

½ C Olive oil
¼ C Fresh lemon juice
1 tsp Red wine vinegar
2 tsp Sugar
1 tsp Salt
½ tsp Ground mustard
½ tsp Worcestershire sauce
¼ tsp Pepper
2 Garlic cloves, minced

Mix all ingredients together in a tightly covered container.

Refrigerate at least 1 hour before serving.

Macaroni Salad

1 pkg Gluten Free garden pagoda pasta
1 C Chopped celery
1 C Cubed ham
1 C Cubed colby jack cheese
1 2¼ oz can Sliced olives
¼ C Peas
¼ tsp Celery salt
½ tsp Garlic salt
1¼ C Gluten free ranch dressing

Cook the pasta according to packages directions.

In a large bowl mix together the celery, ham, cheese, olives, and peas. Mix well.

Next, add the celery salt, garlic salt, and the ranch dressing. Stir until evenly coated.

Drain pasta. Add to the salad and stir well.

Chill 1 hour before serving.

Oregon Potato Salad

7 Medium potatoes, cubed
2 C Sweet pickles, chopped
1 Medium onion, chopped
½ C Pickle juice
1 ½ C Mustard
¾ C Mayonnaise
1 Garlic clove, minced
2 tsp Garlic salt
¼ tsp Pepper
5 Hard boiled eggs, shelled and sliced
Paprika

Place 4 cups of water into a large pot over medium heat. Bring to a boil. Peel all of the potatoes, chop into cubes, and place in the pot once the water is boiling. Cook until potatoes are tender.

In a small pot, over medium heat, bring 2 cups of water to a boil. Place the 5 eggs into the boiling water. Cook for 15 minutes. De-shell the eggs and set aside.

In a large mixing bowl, combine 1 cup of chopped onions, minced garlic, 2 cups sweet pickles, ½ cup of pickle juice, 1 ½ cups mustard, ¾ cups mayonnaise, 2 tsp. garlic salt, 3 sliced hard boiled eggs, and ¼ tsp. pepper. Mix well.

Oregon Potato Salad
Continued

Drain the potatoes when they are tender. Add the potatoes to the mixing bowl and beat on low for 2-3 minutes.

When the potato salad is thoroughly mixed, transfer to a large serving bowl. Dust the top with paprika and place the remaining slices of the hardboiled egg on top.

Refrigerate at least 2 hours before serving.

Raspberry Vinaigrette

½ C Fresh raspberries
¼ C Balsamic vinegar
¼ C Olive oil
1 tsp Sugar
⅛ tsp Garlic, minced

Place all ingredients into a chopper or blender and mix 2 to 4 minutes.

Serve over any salad or use as a vegetable dip.

Roasted Garlic Dipping Sauce

6 Garlic cloves, chopped
1 tsp Salt
2 TBS Olive oil
1 TBS Parsley
½ tsp Thyme
½ tsp Rosemary
Olive oil

Sauté all of the ingredients until garlic turns a golden brown.

Place on a small plate and drizzle olive oil on the plate, about ¼ C.

Serve as an appetizer with bread.

Strawberry Vinaigrette

4 C Strawberries, frozen
4 C Olive oil
1 C Balsamic vinegar
1 TBS Sugar
2 Garlic cloves, minced
2 tsp Pepper

Defrost strawberries.

Mix together the remaining ingredients in a blender. Gradually add the strawberries to the oil mixture.

Serve with any salad. Mix well before serving.

Taco Salad

2 pkg Ground beef
1 TBS Onion powder
1 tsp Garlic salt
2 tsp Paprika
¾ tsp Pepper
1½ tsp Chili powder
¾ C Water
1 Head of iceberg lettuce, shredded
2 C Shredded cheddar cheese
1 Tomato, diced
1 Bag Doritos Tortilla chips
1 Small can sliced olives
1 Can kidney beans
1 Can garbanzo beans
2 Bottles of Walden Farms Gluten Free Thousand Island salad
dressing
Sour cream
Salsa

Brown the ground beef, then add the onion powder, garlic salt,
paprika, pepper, chili powder, and water. Stir well and simmer
for 10 minutes.

In a large bowl, mix together the shredded lettuce, cheese,
tomatoes, ¾ of the Doritos bag, crushed, olives, kidney beans,
and garbanzo beans.

Add the seasoned ground beef to the large salad bowl and stir
until everything is evenly distributed. Pour in the 2 bottles of
thousand island salad dressing and mix well. Garnish with the
remaining tortilla chips, sour cream, and salsa.

Waldorf Salad

⅓ C Mayonnaise
1 TBS Lemon juice
1 TBS Milk
2 Red apples, unpeeled, cored, and coarsely chopped
2 Celery stalks, chopped
1 C Seedless grapes
1 C Scallions, chopped
2 TBS Dried cranberries
⅓ C Walnuts, chopped
Salad greens

In a large bowl, mix the mayonnaise, lemon juice, and milk.

Stir in the apples, celery, grapes, scallions, cranberries, and walnuts. Mix thoroughly.

Serve on salad greens, if desired.

STEWS & SOUPS

Asian Mushroom Soup

Beef Stew

Chicken Noodle Soup

Chicken Soup

Chili

Clam Chowder

Cream of Broccoli & Cheese Soup

Minestrone

Potato Soup

Pumpkin Soup

Tomato Soup

Tortilla Soup

Vegetarian Chili

Asian Mushroom Soup

4 C Chicken broth
2 C Sliced mushrooms, fresh
5 Scallions, chopped
1 C Bean sprouts
Salt and pepper to taste

In a large stockpot, over medium heat, combine all ingredients.

Stir well and cook, stirring occasionally, for 20 minutes.

Serve immediately.

Beef Stew

1-2 lbs Beef stew meat
¼ C Extra virgin olive oil
1 Onion, sliced
4 C Beef broth
2 C Carrots, chopped
4-5 Potatoes, peeled and cubed
1½ C Celery, chopped
1 can Corn, drained
1 C Baby portobello mushrooms
¼-½ C Corn starch
3-5 tsp Kosher salt
Pepper to taste
1 TBS Garlic powder
1 TBS Onion powder
½ tsp Rosemary
½ tsp Basil

In a large skillet, over medium heat, sauté the onion in the olive oil. Add the stew meat and cooked until brown on all sides.

In a crock pot, add the remaining ingredients. Add the stew meat to the stew. Stir well.

More or less corn starch may be used to reach the desired consistency.

Cook on low for 6 hours or high for 3 hours. Stir occasionally.

Chicken Noodle Soup

4 Chicken breasts, cooked and cut into 1 in. strips
2 C Chicken broth
4 C Water
1 Onion, chopped
2 Potatoes, chopped
1 C Carrots, chopped
3 Garlic cloves, minced
½ Box Gluten Free spaghetti
Salt and pepper to taste

In a large pot, over medium heat, place the chicken broth and water.

Add the chopped onion, potatoes, carrots, and garlic. Stir. Then add the chicken. Cook for 30-45 minutes. Add the spaghetti. Cook until noodles are tender.

Serve immediately.

Chicken Soup

4 C Chicken broth
2 C Water
2 C Chicken, cooked and shredded
3 Celery stalks, chopped
2 C Carrots, chopped
1 C Portobello mushrooms, sliced
6 Whole cherry tomatoes
1 Potato chopped
1 TBS Onion powder
1 tsp Pepper
1 tsp Garlic salt
Salt and pepper to taste

Place the chicken broth and water into a large pot over medium heat. Add the celery, carrots, mushrooms, tomatoes, and potatoes. Then add the chicken, onion powder, pepper, and garlic salt.

Cook for 45 minutes, stirring occasionally. Serve immediately.

Chili

1 lb. Ground beef
½ Medium onion
2 Garlic cloves
1 15 oz Can tomato sauce
1 14.5 oz Can diced tomatoes
1 14.5 oz Can stewed tomatoes
1 TBS Chili powder
½ tsp Cumin
1 15 oz Can kidney beans
Sour cream
Shredded cheddar cheese
½ C diced onion

Brown the ground beef together with the onion and garlic.

Place tomato sauce, diced tomatoes, and stewed tomatoes into a large pot.

Add ground beef to the tomato mix.

Add chili powder, cumin, and simmer over medium low heat for 1 hour, stirring occasionally.

Add kidney beans and cook for an additional 10 minutes.

Garnish chili with diced tomatoes, cheese, and sour cream if desired.

Clam Chowder

5 Potatoes, cubed
1 Onion, chopped
3 C Water
½ lb. Bacon
3 tsp. Kosher salt
1 tsp. Pepper
1 Can Baby clams, drained
3 Cans Chopped clams, drained
2 C Half and half
2 C Milk
3 TBS Potato starch
Parsley to garnish

Place the bacon and onions in a large skillet and sauté until golden brown.

Place the water in a large pot. Add the potatoes, salt, and pepper.

Pour the onions and clams into the large pot and stir. Cook over medium heat for one hour, stirring occasionally.

Stir in the half and half, milk, and potato starch. Cook for an additional thirty minutes, stirring occasionally.

Garnish with parsley and serve immediately.

Cream of Broccoli & Cheese Soup

1 Onion, chopped
4 Garlic cloves, minced
2 TBS Butter
3 TBS Tapioca flour
4 C Chicken broth
5 C Fresh broccoli, chopped
5 Potatoes, peeled and cubed
½ C Milk
1 C Cheddar cheese, shredded
1 tsp Kosher salt
½ tsp Pepper

In a large pot, cook the onion and garlic together with the butter until tender. Add the tapioca starch and cook for 3-5 minutes, stirring frequently.

Add the chicken broth. Bring to a boil then add the broccoli and potatoes. Reduce heat and simmer for 15 minutes, or until vegetables are tender.

Strain 1½ cups of the cooked broccoli out of the soup. Place in a food processor or blender until it's evenly chopped. Add the chopped broccoli to the soup along with the milk, cheese, salt, and pepper.

Cook for an additional 15 minutes, stirring occasionally. Serve immediately.

Minestrone

2 TBS Extra virgin olive oil
1 Red onion, finely chopped
2 Carrots, peeled and diced
2 Celery stalks, diced
⅛ tsp Red pepper flakes
¼ tsp Rosemary
1 can Diced tomatoes
2 Potato, peeled and diced
½ lb Green cabbage, finely shredded
2 zucchini, diced
1 C Green beans, fresh and trimmed into 1 inch pieces
2 Garlic cloves, minced
2½ C Chicken broth
2 C Water
1 can Garbanzo beans, drained
Parsley
Parmesan cheese for topping

In a large pot, sauté the onions, carrots, and celery in the olive oil. Stir in the red pepper flakes and rosemary. Cook until the vegetables are caramelized.

Stir in the tomatoes, potatoes, green cabbage, zucchini, green beans, and garlic cloves. Add the chicken broth and water. Bring to a boil, reduce heat, cover and simmer for 20 minutes.

Add the garbanzo beans and simmer for an additional 20 minutes or until vegetables are tender.

Parsley and Parmesan cheese may be used as toppings. Serve immediately.

Potato Soup

6 Potatoes, diced and cooked
3 Celery stalks, chopped
1 Onion, finely chopped
½ C Butter
8 C Milk
¼ C Water
2 C Chicken broth
4 TBS Cornstarch
2 tsp Salt
1 tsp Pepper

Sauté the celery and onion in the butter until onions reach a golden brown color.

Add the milk to the celery mixture and bring to a boil. Stir in the cornstarch.

In a large stock pot, add the celery mixture, water, chicken broth, salt, and pepper. Simmer for 30-45 minutes, over medium heat, stirring as the soup thickens.

Add the potatoes and simmer for another 15 minutes.

Serve immediately.

Pumpkin Soup

2 Cans Pumpkin
4 Potatoes, peeled and cubed
2 Garlic cloves, minced
⅓ C Onions, finely chopped
1 tsp Salt
2-3 C Chicken broth
¼ C Sour cream
½ C Milk
¼ tsp Pepper
½ tsp Parsley

In a large saucepan, combine the pumpkin, potatoes, garlic, and onions. Add the salt and enough broth to barely cover the vegetables, about 2-3 cups.

Cook for 40 minutes, over medium heat, or until the potatoes are soft.

Stir in the sour cream, milk, and pepper. Cook for an additional 15 minutes.

Garnish with parsley and serve immediately.

Tomato Soup

2 TBS Butter
2 TBS Olive oil
2 Onion, sliced
6 Tomatoes, very ripe, peeled, and cut into eights
1 can Tomato paste
1 TBS Basil
1 tsp Thyme
½ tsp Celery salt
1 C Chicken broth
1½ C Water
2 tsp Salt
¼ tsp Pepper

In a large skillet, heat the butter and olive oil until the butter melts. Add the onions and sauté. Stir in the tomatoes, tomato paste, basil, thyme, and celery salt. Smash the tomatoes with a masher.

Stir in the chicken broth and water and bring to a boil, reduce heat, then cover and simmer for 45 minutes.

Using a food processor or blender, puree the soup. Place the pureed soup back into the saucepan and stir in the salt and pepper. Heat until hot and serve immediately.

Tortilla Soup

2 TBS Olive oil
1 Onion, chopped
1 Jalapeno, seeds removed and chopped
2 Garlic cloves, minced
2 Cans Stewed tomatoes
1 Can Beef broth
1 Can Tomato sauce
1 Can Chicken broth
1½ C Water
1 tsp Salt
1 tsp Sugar
1 tsp Cumin
1 TBS Chili powder
½ tsp Lemon pepper
1 tsp Tabasco sauce
2 tsp Worcestershire sauce
3 Chicken breasts, cooked and shredded
12 Corn tortillas, cut into strips

Mix all ingredients together, except for the corn tortillas, in a large pot. Simmer on low for 1 hour.

Add the corn tortilla strips to the soup and serve immediately. Garnish with avocados, sour cream, and/or cheese.

Vegetarian Chili

2½ C Raw kidney beans
1 C Quinoa
1 C Tomato juice
4 Cloves garlic, crushed
1½ C Onion, chopped
1 C Celery, chopped
1 C Carrots, chopped
1 C Green peppers, chopped
2 C Tomatoes, chopped
Juice of ½ a lemon
1 tsp Ground cumin
1 tsp Basil
1 tsp Chili powder
Salt to taste
Pepper to taste
3 TBS Tomato paste
3 TBS Dry red wine
Dash of cayenne
3 TBS Olive oil

Place kidney beans in a sauce pan and cover them with 6 cups of water. Soak for 3-4 hours. Drain and return to pan. Add 6 more cups of water and 1 tsp of salt. Cook for an hour or until tender. Add more water if necessary.

Bring tomato juice to a boil. Pour over the quinoa. Cover and let stand for 15 minutes.

Vegetarian Chili
Continued

Sauté the onions and garlic in the olive oil. Add the carrots, celery, and the spices. When vegetables are almost done, add the peppers. Cook until tender.

Combine all ingredients in a large pot and cook for 30 minutes.

Serve with cheese and parsley.

VEGETABLES

Drunken Carrots

Eggplant Parmesan

Grilled Baked Potato

Horseradish Mashed Potatoes

Loaded Mashed Potatoes

Potato Pancakes

Roasted Herb Potatoes

Rosemary Spinach

Sautéed Asparagus

Sautéed Zucchini and Yellow Squash

Scalloped Potatoes

Steamed Broccoli and Carrots

Stuffed Bell Peppers

Sweet Potato Casserole

Drunken Carrots

1½ lbs Carrots, cut lengthwise into strips
⅓ C Brown sugar, packed
2 TBS Butter
1 tsp Salt
½ tsp Orange Zest
¼ C White wine

In a small saucepan, bring 1 inch of water to a boil. Add carrots. Heat to boiling, reduce heat. Simmer, uncovered, for 10 minutes.

Drain the carrots.

In a medium skillet, add the brown sugar, butter, salt, orange zest, and white wine. Cook to boiling, stirring constantly.

Stir in carrots. Cook over low heat for 5 minutes, stirring occasionally, until carrots are glazed and hot.

Serve immediately.

Eggplant Parmesan

1 Eggplant
4 Eggs, beaten
½ C Gluten free breadcrumbs
1 tsp Italian seasoning
⅓ C Parmesan cheese
½ tsp Garlic salt
¼ C Olive oil
1 C Ricotta cheese
3 C Classic spaghetti sauce
1 C Mozzarella cheese, shredded

Set oven to 350°.

Slice the eggplant into ½ inch strips.

Place 3 beaten eggs in a bowl and set aside.

In a bowl, mix the breadcrumbs with the Italian seasoning. Set aside.

Mix the ricotta cheese and the remaining egg together. Set aside.

Dip the eggplant into the beaten eggs, then into the breadcrumb mixture.

In a pan, over medium-low heat, add the oil then the eggplant. Fry until brown on both sides.

Eggplant Parmesan
Continued

Place half of the eggplant strips in a 9x13 casserole dish. Place half of the ricotta mixture on the eggplant strips. Then place half of the spaghetti sauce over the ricotta mix. Sprinkle with mozzarella cheese. Repeat the layers.

Cook for 45-55 minutes. Serve immediately.

Grilled Baked Potato

1 Potato
2 TBS Butter
½ tsp Garlic salt
Foil

Wash all potatoes.

Slice the potato several times, horizontally. Place the potato on a piece of foil (big enough to wrap the entire potato). Rub the butter on the potato, making sure it gets into the slices. Sprinkle the garlic salt onto the potato. Wrap the potato with foil, making sure the butter won't leak.

Place on grill or in oven for 35 minutes.

Remove from grill or oven and carefully remove the foil. Serve immediately.

Horseradish Mashed Potatoes

5 Potatoes
1¼ C Sour cream
2 tsp Garlic salt
¼ tsp Pepper
1 tsp Onion powder
3 tsp Horseradish
1½ tsp Parsley
2 TBS Butter, softened

Bring 2 quarts of water to a boil.

Rinse and cut the potatoes into small cubes. Place potatoes into boiling water. Cook until potatoes are tender.

Drain the cooked potatoes and return to pan. Stir in the sour cream, garlic salt, onion powder, pepper, and parsley. Mix in the horseradish and the butter. Serve immediately.

Loaded Mashed Potatoes

3 Potatoes, cubed
3 C Water
4 TBS Butter
1 Onion, chopped
3 pcs Bacon, chopped
¼ C Sour cream
1 tsp Parsley

Sauté 1 TBS of butter, the onion, and the bacon in a skillet over medium heat.

Meanwhile, boil the water, and then add the potatoes. Cook until tender.

When the potatoes are finished, drain and then return to pot. Add 3 TBS butter, sour cream, parsley, and the sautéed onions. Mix well.

Serve immediately.

Potato Pancakes

4 Potatoes, peeled
4 Eggs, beaten
1 Onion, finely chopped
¼ C All purpose gluten free flour
1 tsp Salt
¼ C Vegetable oil

Shred the potatoes, rinse, drain, and pat dry.

Mix potatoes, eggs, onion, gluten free flour, and salt in a large bowl.

Heat 2 tablespoons of oil in a large skillet over medium heat. For each pancake, pour ¼ C potato batter into the skillet. Using a large spatula, flatten into the shape of a pancake.

Cook pancakes for 3 minutes on each side or until golden brown. Cover to keep warm while the remaining pancakes are being cooked. Repeat until there is no more batter. Add oil as needed to prevent sticking.

Serve immediately with sour cream, scallions, and/or cheese.

Roasted Herb Potatoes

1 pkg Baby fingerling potatoes
⅓ C Extra virgin olive oil
6 Garlic cloves, minced
1 tsp Basil
1 tsp Parsley
½ tsp Oregano

Set oven to 350°.

Place the potatoes in a 9x9 baking dish.

In a small bowl, add the olive oil, garlic, basil, parsley, and oregano. Stir well.

Drizzle the spices over the potatoes. Stir the potatoes to ensure all over coating.

Cook for 30-45 minutes, or until potatoes are soft.

Serve immediately.

Rosemary Spinach

1 lb. Spinach leaves, fresh
2 TBS Butter
1 tsp Parsley
1 Garlic clove, minced
¼ tsp Rosemary, fresh and crushed

Tear the spinach into bite sized pieces. Rinse well.

Simmer the spinach, in a saucepan, in a small amount of water for 4 minutes. Drain well.

Melt the butter in the saucepan. Add the spinach, parsley, garlic, and rosemary. Sauté for 2 minutes or until the spinach is heated throughout.

Serve immediately.

Sautéed Asparagus

1 bundle Asparagus
¼ C Extra virgin olive oil
2 TBS Kosher salt

In a large skillet, sauté the asparagus in the extra virgin olive oil on low heat. Sprinkle 1 tablespoon of kosher salt on the asparagus.

Cook slowly, turning occasionally, for 15 minutes.

Add the remaining tablespoon of kosher salt, stir, and remove from heat.

Serve immediately.

Sautéed Zucchini and Yellow Squash

2 C Zucchini, sliced
2 C Squash, sliced
⅓ C Extra virgin olive oil
2 Garlic cloves, minced
½ tsp Cinnamon
Salt to taste
Pepper to taste

In a large skillet, over medium heat, add the extra virgin olive oil. Add the zucchini, squash, garlic, cinnamon, salt, and pepper.

Sauté over medium heat for 8-10 minutes, stirring occasionally.

Serve immediately.

Scalloped Potatoes

1 C Sour cream
4 TBS Butter, melted
¼ C Scallions, chopped
1½ C Cheddar cheese, shredded
3 lbs Potatoes, peeled, boiled, and cubed
1 tsp Salt
1 tsp Pepper

Set oven to 350°.

In a large bowl, mix the sour cream, butter, scallions, and 1 C of the cheddar cheese. Gradually stir in the potatoes, salt, and pepper.

Transfer to a 9x9 baking dish. Sprinkle the remaining cheddar cheese on top of the potato casserole.

Bake for 30-35 minutes.

Steamed Broccoli and Carrots

2 C Broccoli, fresh and chopped
2 C Carrots chopped
2 tsp Kosher salt
2 tsp Cayenne pepper

Place a steamer in a medium saucepan. Add water but do not let the water cover the bottom of the steamer.

Add the broccoli, carrots, 1 teaspoon kosher salt, and 1 tsp cayenne pepper. Mix well.

Steam vegetables, covered, for 15 minutes or until vegetables are tender.

Add the remaining kosher salt and cayenne pepper. Mix well and remove from heat. Keep the vegetables covered off of the heat for 2-3 minutes. Serve immediately.

Stuffed Bell Peppers

1 lb Lean ground beef
1 Onion, finely chopped
1 TBS Olive oil
1 can Stewed tomatoes
½ C Rice, cooked
2 TBS Worcestershire sauce
6 Bell peppers, green, red, or yellow
1 C Sharp cheddar cheese, shredded
½ tsp Salt
¼ tsp Pepper

Set oven to 350°.

Brown the ground beef and the onion in the olive oil. Add the stewed tomatoes, cooked rice, and Worcestershire sauce to the browned ground beef.

Cut the tops off of the bell peppers and remove all seeds. Cook the peppers in salted water until boiling, then drain.

Stuff the meat mixture into the bell peppers and place on a baking sheet. Cook, covered, for 40 minutes.

Remove from oven and sprinkle the cheddar cheese on top of all stuffed bell peppers. Return to oven, baking only until the cheese in melted.

Serve immediately.

Sweet Potato Casserole

5 Sweet potatoes
1 C Brown sugar
1 Stick of butter
1 C Pecans, chopped
1 C Shredded coconut

Boil the sweet potatoes in a large pot until tender.

Drain the potatoes when finished, and then remove the skin. Mash the potatoes in the large pot.

Set oven to 350°.

In a 9x9 baking dish, place a layer of potatoes, 4 pats of butter, ⅓ C brown sugar, ⅓ C pecans, and ⅓ C coconut. Repeat the layering until all ingredients are in the casserole.

Cook for 30 minutes.

Serve immediately or refrigerate overnight for next day serving.

Resources

Internet

General information: www.celiac.com- A comprehensive website that addresses all issues a celiac may encounter.

General information: www.celiac.org- A comprehensive website that informs, assists, and supports people who have been diagnosed with celiac disease.

General information: www.csaceliacs.org- A comprehensive website that educates individuals about celiac disease and dermatitis herpetiformis.